101

shortcuts to

relaxation

101

shortcuts to
relaxation

cathy hopkins

BLOOMSBURY

First published in 1997
Bloomsbury Publishing plc
38 Soho Square
London, WIV 5DF

© Cathy Hopkins 1997

Cathy Hopkins has asserted her moral rights.

A copy of the CIP entry for this book is available
from the British Library
ISBN 0 7475 3130 7

10 9 8 7 6 5 4 3 2

Designed by Chris Patmore
Typeset by Hewer Text Composition Services, Edinburgh
Printed in England by Clays Ltd, St Ives plc

In fighting and in everyday life,
you should be determined though calm.
Meet the situation without tenseness
yet not recklessly,
your spirit settled yet unbiased.

Miyanoto Musashi (A Book of 5 Rings:
strategy for a Samurai, 1645)

INTRODUCTION

We are called human beings. *Hu* is a Greek word meaning divine. Divine man being. Yet can many of us honestly say that we know how to *be*? Rather, we are humans doing, humans driving, humans cleaning, humans working, humans hoovering – rarely are we humans relaxing or simply just being.

When I began to research this book, I started by asking around generally to find out what methods people use to relax. Alcohol, cigarettes, drugs, valium, shopping, ice-cream, watching telly, two weeks in the Caribbean came the answers. So much for practical help from friends and acquaintances!

The truth is that when it comes to relaxation, most people want a quick, pleasurable or easy fix which is why a gin and tonic and a cigarette are more often the choice rather than healthy non-addictive solutions.

Sadly, however, the immediate and quick methods we're all familiar with may work temporarily but in the long run can be either unhealthy, addictive, expensive or illegal; other options such as a holiday in the sun or a week in a health farm may well recharge a battery but aren't always possible financially or timewise.

And yet, in a time when the dangers of stress are becoming more and more widely recognized, so, in relation, a wealth of anti-stress techniques, remedies and treatments from different countries and different eras have become more available nationwide. Often the only block between the stressed and the solution is having the time to investigate and discover what's out there.

In researching this book, I've done the time-consuming part for you. Bearing in mind that people don't want long-winded or complicated instructions to add to an already busy day and being aware that when it comes to relaxation, one man's meat is another man's poison, I've found

101 different ways to relaxation. There's something for everyone in here, none of the methods are difficult, many are extremely pleasurable and all are easily applicable in everyday life; plus, they will all contribute to having a healthy and relaxed body and state of mind.

THE IMPORTANCE OF RELAXATION

At one point in my life, I taught meditation for a few years and spent some time in South Africa. One incident always comes back to me – it was when a business man came to see me in his lunch break.

We were due to meet at 12 o'clock. At 12.15, a car roared up and a rather harassed man leapt out and came towards me. In his right hand, he had a sandwich which he proceeded to eat as we spoke.

'OK,' he said, looking at his watch. 'I'm a very busy man and I got another meeting at 1 pm. I can give you half an hour, can you teach me to meditate in that time?'

'I doubt it,' I said, 'but we can certainly talk about it in that time. But relax a bit first. Finish your sandwich. How is it by the way?'

'OK,' he mumbled through the last bites of it.

'Cheese or chicken?'

'Do you know,' he laughed suddenly, 'I haven't a clue.'

If ever a man needed to stop for a moment, it was this one; he was speeding so fast he didn't even know what he was eating. He was already on to the next thing, thinking about his one o'clock meeting while already running late for his present meeting.

It's all too easy to get into this state – tubes not running on time, traffic, pressures, responsibilities all piling up and before you know it you're speeding away, eating on route, planning, forecasting, trying to get ahead, stay on top and hoping to snatch some time off at the weekend. Then that comes round and it's shopping, cleaning, catching up on chores left from the week. Sounds familiar? Time for relaxation, you must be joking. When? How? The answer's now.

We're all under stress of varying degrees, there's no avoiding it in this day and age. Yet what we *do* avoid is doing anything about it, because so many of us are well trained in coping, soldiering on, having a stiff upper lip;

plus, we tell ourselves there's plenty of others more in need. Not true. Everyone needs time to relax.

If on a journey you were unsure about which direction to go in, the first step to finding your way would be to admit that you were lost. In the same way, one of the first steps to relaxation is to admit that you're under stress and do need to take time to unwind.

All sorts of everyday circumstances are taking their toll, depleting energy and inhibiting maximum performance. The list is long and probably familiar: finances, relationships, loss, children, separation, exams, pressure to succeed, work, frustration or job dissatisfaction, being in a hurry, illness, retirement, having a new baby, enforced change, temperature changes, physical stresses, not to mention the evening news with its frequent accounts of daily atrocities around the world.

In the meantime, our health and state of mind is put on the back burner and can often suffer because of it, developing from uncomfortable symptoms and minor inconveniences into more serious problems if not dealt with early on. Arthritis, cardiovascular disease, respiratory disease, cancer and depression are now known to be often stress-related.

Our body is equipped to deal with a certain amount of stress, and in fact some stress can be seen as positive: apprehension before a job interview; stress if something happens to anyone around us; life-threatening situations. We need stress for survival and to be able to deal with anxious times. It is only when the stressful situations are prolonged to the point that they seem uncontrollable and last for months or even years that problems can arise.

When under threat, the hypothalamus in the brain is stimulated. This is the part of the brain that controls our autonomic nervous system, which is composed of two branches, the sympathetic and the parasympathetic. The sympathetic gets us ready to act when in a threatening situation and prepares the body for 'fight or flight'. It does this by increasing the body's energy, raising the heartbeat, increasing the flow of blood to muscles and organs, increasing blood pressure and breathing, increasing sweating and inhibiting the secretion of digestive juices. When the threat is over, the parasympathetic branch of the nervous system calms the body by decreasing the heart rate, decreasing blood flow to organs and muscles, slowing breathing again, lowering blood pressure, stimulating the digestive system and relaxing muscles so that the body returns to normal.

However, in this day and age, the threats and stressful situations we meet tend to last for long periods of time so the parasympathetic branch never really gets the chance to help the body recover. A drawn-out divorce, pressure at work, financial problems, illness and so on are often not situations that can be dealt with in an instant. Hence we are often in fight or flight mode with the sympathetic system getting the body ready to deal with threats that are all around, yet frequently, because of the nature of the situations, we have neither the capacity nor control to do either.

This needn't be a problem. It doesn't mean you have no control, as all you have to do is simply allow time on a regular basis for recovery and for the parasympathetic branch to do its job.

If you can recognize that just as the sympathetic and parasympathetic parts of the nervous system are two sides of the same coin and need to be in balance for good health, with neither being dominant for prolonged periods of time, so in a similar way stress and relaxation can be seen as two sides of the same coin. Stress isn't so much the problem. It is a fact of life we all live with. The problem is when people choose to ignore stress and flog their systems to carry on with no time to catch their breath. The body and mind need time to recover from the ongoing stress or threats all around us.

It can't be emphasized enough that regular time for recovery is the solution to stress and should be seen to be a priority, a necessity in this day and age, and not an indulgence.

We take our car in to be serviced regularly, we expect that it will regularly need some attention and fine-tuning, but when it comes to the vehicle of our own body and mind, it's all too easy to neglect ourselves and expect to carry on regardless.

For improved quality of life on every level, it's important to give the body a chance to unwind, be realigned, pampered, soothed, re-energized. Time to recover. You'll perform all the better for it!

Read through the following checklist of symptoms of stress and if any strike a chord, you need to take some time and thought for your own regular service.

STRESS SYMPTOMS CHECKLIST

Anxiety

Apathy

Asthma

Bloating

Depression

Drug abuse

Excessive drinking or smoking

Exhaustion

Fatigue

Fear

Feeling run-down

Forgetfulness

Headaches

Herpes

High blood pressure

Increased adrenaline

Increased heart rate

Increased perspiration

Insomnia

Irritable bowel syndrome

Irritability

Lack of sex drive

Loss of appetite

Loss of concentration

Migraine

Muscle tension

Neck and back pain

Palpitations

Premature ageing

Shallow breathing

Short-tempered

Teeth-grinding during the night

Tight tense stomach

Trembling hands

Ulcers

Weakened immune system and tendency to come down with every bug or virus going round

Weight loss or gain

Withdrawn

If any of the above look familiar then you'll benefit from looking at the ways outlined in the book to aid relaxation.

STATE OF MIND CAN DETERMINE YOUR WHOLE LIFE

It's an interesting phenomenon in life, that when we look back at episodes gone by we can see clearly how our past experience is often made up not so much of the events that have happened to us but of our response and reaction to them; i.e. how we were feeling about life at the time. For example, a holiday in the sun can be a dream or a nightmare depending on the state of mind that we're in. External factors that may be close to paradise do not necessarily equal a good time if we feel lousy or stressed inside.

A week at work can be a pleasure or a pain, again depending on how we're feeling within. A traffic jam can be a temporary inconvenience or the last straw.

Our inner frame of mind is very important to our quality of life, yet often little is done to cultivate an internal state of balance; it's more likely we try to 'fix' the external factors instead. We redecorate, move house, get a hair cut, new clothes, take a holiday, form a new relationship but it somehow doesn't always lead to the end we envisaged.

This book is about how to achieve the life you want. Like the saying 'take care of the pennies and the pounds will take care of themselves', in the same way, pay attention to your frame of mind, health and well-being, and it will often follow that the externals will take care of themselves, or at least the significance of everything having to be 'right' on the outside diminishes. If you feel happy inside you can be anywhere and it seems like the perfect place to be.

You can't manufacture happiness by trying to make everything all right on the outside. Christmas is the classic example: time off, an abundance of gifts, food, drink and being surrounded by our loved ones does not, as many of us know only too well, result in a guaranteed happy time.

TIPS FROM DIFFERENT APPROACHES

There is never one secret ingredient or key as a solution to peace of mind; rather, it is an art, a conscious combining of several approaches that take into account the many levels which affect us as human beings. The physical, the emotional, the mental, the nutritional, the environmental and the spiritual must all be given time and attention for true and lasting tranquillity. On the path to relaxation, one part of us cannot be ignored in favour of another, which is why this book will incorporate advice from all of these areas. It will also outline some of the wonderful treatments, therapies and advice now available to help the process along.

There has never before been time when the wealth of knowledge from the ancient and modern worlds of other cultures, plus that of our own, has been so accessible: through a general awareness of the availability of alternative treatments in local health shops, clinics and bookshops, the time has never been better for achieving relaxation.

The shortcuts outlined in the book dip into seven different approaches to combating stress and are well within the realms of possibility for anyone with or without a busy schedule.

THE SEVEN APPROACHES IN THE BOOK

1   Mental (shortcuts numbers 1–13)
- Making choices
- Time management
- Visualizations

2   Physical (shortcuts numbers 14–30)
- Breathing exercises to calm
- Improved posture for prevention of back and neck ache
- Stretches and gadgets for quick relief
- Relaxation positions and exercises

3   Nutritional (shortcuts numbers 31–45)
- Diet
- Vitamins, minerals for stress
- Teas for relaxation

4   Alternative solutions (shortcuts numbers 46–68)
- Short-term 'fixers' – remedies, potions and oils from health shops
- Regular sessions for relaxation such as aromatherapy, shiatsu and reflexology
- DIY massage and relaxation processes

5   Emotional (shortcuts numbers 69–76)
- Emotional release exercises
- Counselling
- Letting off steam: techniques for letting out frustration and anger

6 Environmental (shortcuts numbers 77–88)
  - Gadgets for the home and office (chairs, beds, pillows)
  - Practical suggestions for a stress-free environment

7 Spiritual (shortcuts numbers 89–101)
  - Meditation techniques
  - Prayer
  - The importance of inspiration
  - Inspirational writings

HOW TO USE THIS BOOK

Familiarize yourself with the various different approaches then simply dip in and out using the ways that appeal and considering the benefits of others that are perhaps new to you. As the saying goes, the longest journey starts with the first step so pace yourself. Don't feel you have to try out every way in a few weeks.

Also, stress affects different people in different ways so not all of the shortcuts will be relevant for everyone. Some people have back strain as a result of purely physical stress and will benefit from the physical stretches and advice about posture; others who can't sleep because of emotional stress will get the most out of the techniques for releasing pent-up emotion and taking a herbal remedy for insomnia; others may be stressed and tired due to poor diet and lack of exercise which can be improved by taking vitamin and mineral supplements and looking at their overall lifestyle. The different relaxation techniques outlined in the book will work for different types according to their needs at the time.

I've timed each example given so you can see just how *possible* each one is: some take no longer than the time it takes to breathe; others take five minutes; and some require more time, when, for example, you have to schedule for a pampering session like an aromatherapy massage.

Each way is of value in itself, but combining them with each other will ensure a smooth and rewarding experience in life all round.

DON'T PUT OFF UNTIL TOMORROW
WHAT YOU CAN DO TODAY

Make time out for yourself a priority now. Get out your diary and schedule time off for relaxation, along with all your other priorities. Be realistic and choose times that you know are feasible in your week.

Try to make time daily even if it's just ten minutes. Or weekly, even if it's just an hour. Or monthly, even if it's just an evening. These times may not seem like much but actually they will benefit you greatly, as most people don't actually relax even during their time off or at weekends. Time off is for ironing, charging round the supermarket, entertaining, cooking, cleaning the car . . .

Stress often builds over a period of time to the point where it is debilitating, and remedying stress in ways that are effective requires time and scheduling.

CHOICE NOT CHANCE DETERMINES DESTINY

Choose to relax by making changes to ensure that you have time to unwind in a way that suits you. After reading through the book, decide which methods you are going to try and schedule them in. The choices and decisions that you make today determine your future. Just as the seeds of today become the fruits of tomorrow, in the same way your thoughts and choices of today become your deeds and actions of tomorrow. So choose to make time to relax. This is one of the most important of all the steps to relaxation.

Don't make excuses: No – I would if only I had time. I would but I can't afford it. I will. I will. But tomorrow.

As many of us know too well from a hundred positive resolutions – I'll start on Monday; next week; New Year – so many get put off as our busy lives whizz on consuming us. Who was it that said that the road to hell is paved with good intentions?

Get out your diary and a pen and schedule in definite dates. For example: Tuesday night – visualization to help sleep; Wednesday lunch – try stretches for relieving the back; Saturday morning – aromatherapy massage. Make a shopping list of the remedies or gadgets that sound like they may be useful to you. Allocate an hour to go and get them for the medicine cabinet or for the office. There are addresses at the back of the book in the Useful Addresses section that will tell you where to find a local practitioner and where you can purchase by mail order anything you read about in the book.

Book in treatments today. Even if it's for three weeks ahead. It's in your diary. At the end of each session, make your next appointment, otherwise weeks and months will drift by and it's a case of 'oh I meant to but . . .' If you'd like to try lavender oil or camomile tea, put them on the shopping list now and pin it to the front door so that you get them on your next shopping trip.

NB: In many of the shortcuts throughout the book, I have indicated that you should breathe deeply into the abdomen. To fully comprehend and experience how this feels in order to gain maximum benefit from other techniques and exercises, turn to shortcut 15 in the Physical Shortcuts section.

You can either run through the technique a few times so that you are familiar with how it feels or refer back to it whenever you see 'breathe fully into your abdomen' written.

Mental Shortcuts

1

TIME MANAGE YOUR PRIORITIES

'The past is a cancelled cheque, the future a promissory note.
The present is the only time you have. Spend it wisely.'

TIME: *5–10 minutes*

INGREDIENTS: *paper/pen*

Having a lot to do can result in a feeling of being weighed down and anxious while the tasks needing to be done can blow out of proportion in the mind, leaving a sense of panic and inability to cope. This simple time-management technique can reduce stress by simply getting it all out and down on paper so that you can see exactly what has to be done, prioritize what's urgent and break the rest down into manageable chunks of your time.

METHOD

1 Sit down and make a list of all the things that you have to do in the next day/week/month.

2 Read over your list and start to prioritize. What is most important and can't be put off? Number that as one.

3 Carry on through the list and mark out the top 10 items that have to be done the most urgently then number the remaining tasks in order of importance.

4 Keeping in mind your top 10 items, approximately how long do you envisage each task will take? Mark the time you allot yourself for numbers one to ten on your list.

5 Looking at the time needed, how many can you accomplish today? Go back and mark how ever many you can accomplish in one day without pushing yourself. Mark these with a 'T'.

6 When you start to do a task, finish it. A lot of stress arises because people panic and lose focus. They try to do everything at once and start a bit here and a bit there. This only prolongs the feeling of stress as your mind knows that there's unfinished business. You will accomplish much more if you complete one thing at a time.

7 As you finish a task, delete it from the list.

8 When you have finished your top 10, move on. The next day, take two minutes to mark the tasks of the day with a new T.

It is surprising how simply by writing and breaking down what we need to accomplish, it ceases to panic us. Only when left in the mind, floating around, can it assume the pressure that causes stress and sleepless nights as we keep going over and over what we have to do. Time management allows us to see that we can cope and is an excellent way of reducing stress.

2

MAKE TIME TO WORRY!

TIME: *30–60 minutes*

INGREDIENTS: *diary, pen, three sheets of paper, drawing pin*

This may sound like an odd statement in a book about relaxation where you perhaps thought you were to be told to forget your worries. However, as we all know only too well, worries have a nasty habit of persisting and making their presence felt until we come up with solutions. By actually scheduling time for worry, it lets your mind know that you have heard it and are going to do something about it rather than let the anxiety spin around in your head for 24 hours a day, seven days a week, sometimes causing sleepless nights.

METHOD

1 Get out your diary and schedule in a time to deal with anxieties. Start with giving yourself at least an hour. This will immediately give you some mental reprieve, leaving you free to deal with other demands on your time and energy without the persistent nagging that can go on at the back of your head.

2 At the allotted time, get out three sheets of paper. On page one, write down all the things that are bothering you and that you would like to remedy. Finances, miscommunications, too much work load, relatives and so on. Spend 10 to 15 minutes on this.

3 On page two, divide the paper into two columns. At the head of column one write 'Drawbacks'. Fill in all the reasons why your problem is one and what obstacles are in your way. Spend 10 to 15 minutes on this.

4 At the top of column two, write 'Possible Solutions'.

Opposite each drawback, write down all the possible options, solutions and compromises. Spend 15 to 20 minutes on this, e.g.:

Drawback	Solution
No time to write my novel	Get up an hour earlier
Tired and stressed	Have an early night; book a regular massage
Arguing about holidays	Reasonable compromises
Overdraft growing	Talk to bank manager? Possible loans? Expenditure that can be cut back on?

5 Go back over the list of solutions and number them 1 to 10 (or 20) in order of priority, urgency and possibility and note when you can act on them.

6 On page three, make a new list of your solutions in the order of importance you chose, plus the dates and times you can act on them.

7 Pin this somewhere prominent and act upon it. You'll feel a lot freer and lighter for having dealt with these problems in a constructive way instead of letting them all spin round in your head. In addition, they may not seem so bad once you've got them down on paper.

3

BE PREPARED

TIME: *unlimited*

INGREDIENTS: *variable upon your preparations*

'Be prepared' is the old Scout motto, but it is good advice at any age. There will always be unavoidable times when you can't help but be in a hurry. You can't relax and take it easy. You're under pressure perhaps from an early start, a demanding schedule and a million things to do along the way. This is where the old 'be prepared' motto comes in. You may have to dash but you can ensure that everything goes smoothly and causes minimum stress by organizing yourself in advance on a slow Sunday afternoon or on the night before a hectic day. It may only take 10 minutes, it may take half an hour, but it will help you ride the pressurized times more calmly. It will be worth it because as we all know the more you rush and panic the more things get lost, get dropped, get forgotten, causing the very stress you're aiming to avoid.

METHOD

Put some time aside the next day off you have and list all the areas that cause you to panic and rush and list how you could be prepared. Although everyone's routine and demands on time are different, here's a few examples of the sorts of things that you can do to ensure stress-free running:

1 Lay out work clothes the night before (for you and the kids).

2 Always carry a good book for train and tube delays. A momentary distraction is much better than growing more and more agitated.

3 Keep an A–Z in the car of the city where you live.

4 Label videos of programmes you want to keep as soon as you've recorded them (saves the stress of recording over material you want, or trying to find it again).

5 Have your papers and milk delivered.

6 Keep a set of car and house keys with a neighbour or friend. (A classic symptom of overdoing it is locking the car keys in the car or mislaying keys.)

7 Keep a notepad handy for jotting down 'must do's', rather than letting them spin around in your head adding to rising panic and the stress of knowing there was something you had to do if only you could remember what!

8 Join the AA or RAC.

9 Keep soothing music in the car for times when you're stuck in traffic.

10 Keep desks, drawers and wardrobes clutter-free for easy access when in a hurry.

You get the idea. Forethought is forearmed.

4

RELAX WITH AN AUTOGENIC EXERCISE

TIME: *5–10 minutes*

INGREDIENTS: *cushion to support knees*

Autogenics were devised by a German neurologist Dr Johannes Schultz. He came up with a series of exercises to help patients relax through the silent repetition of certain suggestions. Autogenic comes from a Greek word meaning 'coming from within'; autogenic training consists of a series of simple mental exercises, similar to meditation, designed to help combat stress through inner suggestions of warmth, heaviness and tranquillity which then allow the body to calm and heal itself.

This exercise combines autogenic instructions with relaxation techniques. You can start by running through the process in five minutes and then, as your concentration builds, take longer until the process lasts 20 minutes.

METHOD

1 Either lie down on your back, with support under your knees and head, and close your eyes, or sit comfortably in a chair with your feet apart and parallel. Rest your hands on your thighs, with your head either up or leaning slightly forward. Take a few deep breaths in and out and think to yourself 'I am relaxed and at peace with myself'.

2 Take your attention to your right arm. Silently verbalize the words 'my right arm is heavy'. Think of your right arm. Imagine it being heavy, relaxed, sinking into whatever is supporting it – the chair, bed or floor. Disassociate the arm from the rest of the body. Moments later, internally repeat the phrase again, 'My right arm is heavy'.

Do this a number of times then do the same process with the right leg, left arm, left leg, shoulders, back and neck. Allow at least 30 seconds, more if it feels necessary, for each part of the body.

3 Take yourself through the same process as number two but this time say the words 'my right arm is warm'. As you proceed, visualize your arm/leg becoming warm. Sense warmth as you say the words to yourself. If it helps, imagine the sun shining down warming the skin and spreading through to the whole arm.

Go through the whole body – arms, legs, neck, shoulders – stopping after each suggestion to allow time for your mind and muscles to relax.

4 This stage focuses on the breath. Say to yourself 'my breathing is calm and regular'. Don't control your breathing, let it happen naturally. Be aware of the movement of your diaphragm as your chest rises and falls, but remain passive, let it happen. You could also think 'I am being breathed' as you note the breathing in and out. Slow repetition of either of these phrases helps regular breathing without any conscious effort on your part.

Continue this stage for several minutes.

5 Now think the following phrase to yourself – 'my forehead is cool'. Repeat it inside yourself several times, pausing after each time to allow yourself to imagine and feel the sensation of coolness on your forehead.

6 In the last stage, think to yourself, 'I am alert and refreshed and at peace'. Take time to feel this. Breathe deeply, acknowledge the sensation of being refreshed and calm then stretch and get up slowly.

5

CREATE YOUR OWN TAILOR-MADE VISUALIZATION TO HELP YOU THROUGH STRESSFUL SITUATIONS

TIME: *5-10 minutes*

INGREDIENTS: *chair*

This technique is one used by NLP practitioners. NLP stands for neuro-linguistic programming and was founded in the early 1970s. It is called neurolinguistic programming because it deals with three main areas. 'Neuro' pertains to the fact that our responses and reactions to life come from the neurological processes of sight, hearing, smell, taste and touch. 'Linguistic' refers to the ways that we communicate through both verbal and non-verbal language. 'Programming' refers to the way in which we choose to behave in life and recognizes that any behaviour has been learnt, e.g. good and bad habits, and therefore can be relearnt or reprogrammed.

NLP is a set of learning skills to enable a person to improve their level of performance by overcoming their limitations. This is done by altering patterns of thought, behaviour and language to help achieve desired goals, reach a more effective level of communication and new levels of competence in, claim NLP practitioners, virtually any area of life's experiences.

NLP recognizes that individuals respond differently to different sensory stimuli. For example, some people respond best to scenes of visual peace, others to sounds that they find calming, others to feelings and others to taste and smell. This simple technique allows for these personal preferences to be taken into account as each person creates their own fantasy.

METHOD

1   Sit comfortably in a chair with your legs uncrossed and your feet flat on the floor. Think back to a situation when you felt the most relaxed. Take your time if you need to think for a moment. When you have recollected such a time, recall the picture of where you were as clearly as you can.

2   Visualize the colours around you. If you like, turn up the brightness of these colours in your recollection.

3   When you have done that, think back. Were there any sounds there that you can recall? If so, hear them in your mind. Turn the sounds up or down if you wish. If it was quiet, recall how that sounded.

4   Next be aware of how you felt. How was your neck? Your body? What sensations were you aware of? Make yourself feel even more relaxed. If you wish, make this sensation of calm even stronger and feel yourself letting go into total relaxation.

5   Were there any tastes at this time? Or perhaps smells? If there were, bring them into the picture.

6   How are you now? Bring the whole picture together with all the sensations and make an action with your hands to recall to yourself this personal visualization of you at your most relaxed. It can be with your hands or fingers, whatever works for you. Clench your hands or make a gesture with your fingers. Once you have this action, it is your personal sign to yourself to recall your visualization.

It is used to trigger a psychological effect to reactivate the sensation of relaxation. You will find that as soon as you do your signal, your brain recalls the relaxed memory and all the sensations that go with it, causing an instant release of tension to take place.

Use this in any situation in which you feel yourself tensing up, for example, before an interview or exam, or during any stressful experience where you know you need to relax.

Many people find this technique particularly useful because it allows every individual to create their own personal relaxation fantasy, and thus one that works to maximum effect for them.

6

RELEASE ALL PHYSICAL TENSION FROM YOUR BODY WITH THIS SIMPLE VISUALIZATION EXERCISE

TIME: *5, 10 or 15 minutes, as long as you like*

INGREDIENTS: *blank cassette, tape recorder, pillow to support knees*

This is an easy visualization used by thousands of people all over the world and is particularly useful if having difficulty unwinding before sleep.

The exercise helps all the muscles in the body relax and is useful because different people hold tension in different parts of their body: some in the jaw, others in the neck, shoulders or lower back, some in the gut, stomach or in their knees. This exercise travels through all the body, consciously encouraging the muscles and organs to let go of knots and tensions unconsciously held there.

METHOD

You can either:

1   read this page through first then think yourself through it;

2   ask someone to slowly read the instructions out loud to you without hurrying, as you follow them in your mind;

3   pre-record yourself or a friend reading through the instructions then switch on your tape, lie back and follow the exercise. Keep the voice slow and soothing.

NB: many people find it more effective and easier to keep concentration and follow if it is a voice reading the instructions out loud. When reading, do so very slowly pausing between sentences to allow internal visualizations and relaxing to happen. Vary the length of pauses from five seconds to ten seconds before moving on to different parts of the body.

THE EXERCISE

1 First lie comfortably in a quiet room where you won't be disturbed. Put a pillow under your knees for support and added comfort.

2 Close your eyes. Take a deep, slow breath in, hold it and let it out with a sigh. Take another slow deep breath in, hold it and let it out with a sigh. Take a third breath in and exhale in your own time.

3 Now take your focus down to your feet. Be aware of them. Is there any tension there? In the toes? In the ankles? Now clench the muscles in your feet tight then consciously let go. Enjoy the sensation of having relaxed feet. When you feel your feet have had enough attention and all tension has gone from them, if you feel ready, move up to the calf muscles.

4 Tighten the muscles in the back of your leg, hold for a moment then relax, feel the muscles let go, easing, relaxing, sinking heavily into the surface below you. Pause for a while to allow this relaxation to take place. Don't hurry it. Feel the muscles letting go, growing heavy . . . Register the sensation of release.

5 When you're ready, move up to the thighs. Clench the muscles tight then let go, release, let them sag, heavy, feel if there is any tension there. Let it go. Let them become weighty, heavy like bags of sand.

If you feel any tensions returning to any of the parts we covered, let it go again. Grow heavier, grow sleepier.

6 Now move up to the buttocks. Clench them tight and release, feeling them sink into the surface below.

Next the lower body. How does it feel? Are you aware of any knots in the lower abdomen? Tense the muscles in this area, hold for a few moments then let them go. Feel them relaxing, unwinding. Pause for a moment while you feel the whole of this area undoing, smoothing out, easing.

7 What about the lower back? Is there any tension there? Tense and let it release. Feel it sink into the surface. Your lower body is heavy, relaxed. Breathe deeply into this area feeling it calming. Easing.

8   When you are ready move up to stomach and solar plexus area. Focus on the area just below your ribcage. How does it feel? Are there any knots there? Tighten them, hold, then feel them undoing, releasing. The area is feeling soothed, calm, relaxed.

9   Go to the middle back, are you holding on there? Feel your lower body sinking into the surface below you, your body feeling heavy, relaxed, all tensions and knots easing away. Feel your breathing calm, regular, easy.

10   When you are ready move to the arms. How do they feel? Tighten the muscles, clench, hold, then release. If there's any tension there, feel it leaving as your arms sink down with relaxed weight. How are your hands? Clench them, tight, make fists, then let them drop uncurled, open and relaxed.

11   When you are ready, move up to your neck and shoulders. Is there any tension there, lingering, holding on? Lift your shoulders up, scrunching towards your ears, tighten, then let them go, drop back down. Feel your neck release, your shoulders sinking into the surface below you. Keep breathing regularly, easily and feel the weight and heaviness of the whole body sinking down, not an area of tension anywhere. Relaxed. Calm. Serene.

12   When you are ready move up to your head. Be aware of your jaw, how does it feel? Clench it, hold, then let it drop heavy, relaxed. Let your lower jaw drop. Scrunch your face muscles up. Now let them relax. Feel your head growing heavy, soothed. Be aware of the forehead, is there tension there? Thoughts? Worries? Let them go. Feel them easing, relaxing. Your whole face feels relaxed, heavy, easy. Become aware of the back of your head, let it drop deeper into the pillow, sinking, heavily relaxed, all tensions giving up now, relaxing, calm.

13   Your whole body is relaxed now, your breathing the only motion, you feel heavy, at ease, serene, calm. Now let yourself sleep or lie in this relaxed state for as long as you like.

7

A VISUALIZATION TO FLOAT STRESS AWAY

TIME: *5 minutes*

INGREDIENTS: *chair or bed*

This visualization is particularly effective if you're having difficulty sleeping because anxieties keep buzzing round in your mind.

METHOD

1 Either lie on your back or sit comfortably, arms and legs uncrossed, feet firmly on the floor.

2 Picture yourself with a bunch of deflated balloons in your hands. Think about various anxieties you have and give them all an appropriate label or name, i.e. finances, work, a person, relationship etc.

3 In your mind, visualize that you are blowing up your first balloon and imagine that you are blowing all your worries about a particular problem into the balloon. See the label clearly imprinted on the balloon material and see it swell as you blow into it. Once you feel all the anxieties about that subject have been blown out, start on the next.

4 Work methodically through all your worries blowing them into the balloons until in your mind you have blown them all out of you.

5 See yourself in a wide open space holding all the balloons in your hand. Now let go of them all and visualize them floating away, high above you, whilst you are left below, relaxed and clear of anxiety.

8

A VISUALIZATION TECHNIQUE TO BRING OUT A MORE POSITIVE AND RELAXED YOU

TIME: *5–10 minutes*

INGREDIENTS: *chair*

This is particularly good for anyone whose imagination or power of visualization is strong.

A visualization or picture is a potent tool to guide the subconscious as many believe that what we imagine can eventually externalize. For example, if someone describes a scene to you, you get an idea of it, but if you see the scene with your own eyes it is so much more memorable and clear. If you feed your subconscious mind positive, visual images, the level of influence is much more effective than trying to tell yourself something with words or affirmations.

The subconscious mind is like a force without direction. Like steam or electricity, it will do what it is told but has no power of induction itself. What we feel deeply, or imagine, is impressed on the subconscious mind to the minutest detail, therefore it must be trained and influenced to manifest what is for our greater and more positive good.

METHOD

1 Sit comfortably, arms and legs uncrossed and feet parallel.

2 Close your eyes and imagine a screen in front of you, either a TV, slide or cinema screen.

3 Visualize that down in the left-hand corner of your screen is an image of yourself at your most stressed and anxious. See yourself, your posture and how you're feeling. Spend a moment or two on this until your picture is as clear as you can get it.

4   Now leave this image and go up to the right-hand top corner of your screen and see yourself at your best. Freshly washed hair, glowing, looking your most radiant, relaxed and enjoying yourself. Note your posture, how you feel. Spend a few moments on this image until it is as clear as you can get it.

5   Now slowly, in your mind, bring the two images together in the middle of your screen but let the image from the top right-hand corner come in front of the one from the left-hand corner.

6   Concentrate on this image of you at your best superimposed on top of the stressed image.

7   Now turn up the volume control on your screen. Put any sound you like into your picture. Then turn up the brightness and colour control. Make the image as vivid and clear as you can.

8   Take a deep breath and when you're ready, open your eyes.

9

A VISUALIZATION TO DISSOLVE STRESS AWAY

TIME: *5 minutes*

INGREDIENTS: *chair*

This visualization uses the power of the mind to heal and relax.

METHOD

1 Sit in a comfortable position in a softly lit room, legs and arms uncrossed, feet firmly on the ground.

2 Scan your body to become aware of where you're holding your tension. Focus to feel if it is in the neck, the lower back, shoulders or knees, in the jaw or solar plexus and stomach area. Scan all these areas.

3 See your body as a vessel or outline full of light but wherever there is tension, visualize it as a shadow or dark dull spot.

4 Now go to the first area where you feel your tension. If it's a shoulder, lift it then let it go limp and heavy. As you relax, see the area getting lighter in your outline image. If it's your jaw that is tight, clench it then let it relax and grow lighter in your inner image as you let go of the tension. Imagine the dark spot on your mental image dissolving away as you let go physically. If your stomach is tense, pull in the muscles and as you let go, see the shadow area grow lighter in your image.

Go through each area, clenching then relaxing, or pulling in and relaxing. As you focus on each tight area, at the same time, in your light image of the body, see the dull dark spots dissolve into the light as the tightness relaxes.

5   When you've finished the body scan, imagine a cloud of golden light all around you. Inhale and imagine that you are breathing in this light right into your abdomen. As you breathe it in, imagine the golden light flooding into all the areas of stress and strain, dissolving and lightening any last residues of discomfort, darkness or shadow. As you breathe out, imagine any remaining stress and tension is being exhaled from your body. Repeat this breathing five to ten times. When you feel that all the dark spots have been completely dissolved by your inhalations of golden light, open your eyes.

10

AN EFFECTIVE VISUALIZATION FOR PRE-INTERVIEW NERVES OR PRE-PRESENTATION ANXIETY

TIME: *5 minutes*

INGREDIENTS: *chair*

This visualization is effective for times that you are dreading and that fill you with fear. Like the prior techniques, this influences the subconscious with a picture of a more relaxed and positive successful you.

METHOD

1 Sit in a comfortable position, with your arms and legs unclosed, and your feet firmly on the floor parallel to each other. Breathe deeply into your abdomen.

2 Visualize a screen – either a TV, slide or cinema screen. Now think about whoever or whatever situation is causing you anxiety, whether it be a meeting with the bank manager, an interview, a presentation, doctor's appointment, teacher, neighbour, friend or relative. See them on your screen. What are they wearing? What's their expression? Are they sitting or standing? Visualize details about them and about where you are. Is it inside or outside? Imagine the scene. Furniture? Plants or flowers? Are there paintings on the wall? Complete your picture until you have it as clear as you can get it.

3 Now shrink the image down slightly on the screen and frame it. As with the picture you've created, now imagine the frame. Is it gold, black or white? Carved wood or plastic? Spend a moment or two on the frame until you have it as clear as you can get it in your mind.

4 Now make your image comical. Change what you like on the picture. Draw a moustache on their face, or a clown's curly wig, or big bags under their eyes and a wide clown's mouth and a big floppy ruff around their neck. Some people imagine the person they are anxious about naked. Draw spectacles on. Whatever you want. Trousers that end above the ankles. A jacket that's way too big or too small. Spend a moment or two changing the picture in the frame until you are satisfied that it no longer fills you with fear and that, in fact, it now looks rather jovial.

5 Now turn up the brightness volume on your screen. See the colours and picture as vividly as you can.

6 Take a deep breath and when you are ready, open your eyes. Next time you encounter either your anxiety or the person that has made you anxious, bring to mind your framed picture. It will immediately lessen the anxiety.

11

A POSITIVE VISUALIZATION TECHNIQUE FOR PRE-PRESENTATION STRESS

TIME: *5 minutes*

INGREDIENTS: *chair*

What can be imagined can happen. First the thought, then the action. If you feed positive imaging into your mind, when you go into the real situation your inner mind will take over to make your inner image come real. It knows what to do.

As with the previous technique, this will help calm nerves before a tense situation. You could try both of them and see which works best for you.

METHOD

1 Sit comfortably.

2 Imagine that you're about to go into your presentation or interview. Recognize the anxiety or butterflies you have and know that this sensation is completely normal. Everyone experiences it before a major performance of any kind, so don't try and suppress it.

3 Now imagine yourself going into the situation you are anxious about. How are you dressed? See yourself. How does the room look? See your surroundings. How are the other people dressed? See them as clearly as you can in your mind.

4 Now see yourself in this situation as being relaxed, calm and completely in control. A success. See them responding to you. Their expressions show that they too are as relaxed as you are. Talk yourself through your presentation and see it being a great success.

You can do this the night before you do your presentation and you can do it again moments before you go in on the actual day. Just as an actor rehearses how a scene is to go in a play, rehearse your preparation in your head so that you are in charge of your performance.

As the following quote says, 'We are what we repeatedly do. Excellence, then, is not an act but a habit.'

You can run through times of potential stress mentally and see yourself as being calm and successful so many times that, in the end, relaxed behaviour in tense situations becomes a part of your make-up, a habit.

12

USE IMAGES OF LIGHT AND WARMTH WITH DEEP BREATHING FOR IMMEDIATE RELAXATION

TIME: *5–10 minutes*

INGREDIENTS: *chair*

Just as negative thoughts and images can create physical symptoms of stress and tension, so positive images can create feelings of serenity and well-being which bring about physical relaxation in the body. This results in a slowing down of the heart rate, lowering of the blood pressure and release of muscular tension.

METHOD

1 Sit comfortably with your back straight, preferably in a room where you are not going to be disturbed or distracted (although once you've mastered this you can practise it on the tube, bus or even before going in for an interview – anywhere that you can shut your eyes for five minutes).

2 Close your eyes and slowly focus your awareness inside of yourself. Be aware of your backside sitting on the chair, the sensation of sitting. Now let your hands gently rest on your abdomen. Become aware of the pattern of your breathing. Now breathe right down into the abdomen feeling how, as you inhale, your hands rise as the abdomen fills out and fall again as you exhale. As you breathe in, start to imagine your abdomen is a balloon that swells as it fills with air and deflates when you exhale. Concentrate on this sensation for a few breaths.

3 When you have got this, start to visualize a sensation of warmth flooding into you as you breathe in. Warmth is filling the balloon in your abdomen. As you breathe out, imagine that all your stress and worry or negativity is being exhaled.

4 Concentrate on this sensation as you breathe in and out for a few more minutes. When you have got this, start to imagine that as you breathe in the warmth, you are also breathing in light. Light is flooding through you, warming you as it is inhaled. Again as you exhale, imagine that all the doubts or dark feelings in you are gently flowing out, leaving you ready to be filled with more light and warmth as you breathe in again.

Continue like this for five to ten minutes. When you feel relaxed and ready to get up, open your eyes and become aware of the room around you. Be aware of how you feel before you dash off, then slowly get up and continue your day.

You will feel relaxed, focused and recharged by this quick, simple exercise.

13

RELAX AS YOU LISTEN TO YOUR OWN VOICE TAKE YOU ON A GUIDED VISUALIZATION

TIME: *10–15 minutes*

INGREDIENTS: *favourite music cassette, cassette recorder, blank cassette*

There are many relaxation tapes available from health shops and centres around the country. They usually combine a guided visualization with some gentle background music to help soothe. As everyone has different preferences, especially when it comes to music, you may or may not find the music on these tapes conducive to relaxation. Also, you may or may not like the voice that guides the visualization. A simple alternative is to make your own.

METHOD

1   First select a piece of music that you find soothing and non-intrusive. You can put this on as you record yourself slowly reading the following visualization. When you have finished, lie back, put the tape on and let your own voice guide you into a state of peace and tranquillity.

2   Test all your equipment. It is important to get your sound levels right and this may take some time and adjusting so experiment before your final read-through. You don't want your voice to be too loud or too quiet, so ensure that you have your microphone or cassette at the right distance away from you before you start your reading. Also be aware of any background noises – planes, kids, traffic, neighbours, dogs barking. You may not notice these sounds when you are reading but you may find them a distraction when you play back your tape. Try to find a quiet room in which to do your recording.

3 Ensure that your music tape is long enough and that if it needs turning over at any point that you are ready for it and can stop and switch it over without it sounding like a major disturbance on your final recording.

4 Make sure your blank tape is long enough for your whole recording. If it has to turn over at some point, have a trial read-through so that you know when to stop. It is better to have a few moments silence at the end of side one rather than to find that you are cut off mid-sentence.

5 Read through the passage a few times so that you are familiar with what is written. Take your time and be aware of your breathing; don't rush through it.

6 When everything is in place, sit in a comfortable position and before you begin, breathe deeply into your abdomen, hold, then breathe out with a sigh. Breathe in deeply again, hold and let go. Breathe in deeply and, this time, breathe out in your own time.

7 Read aloud the following passage into the microphone. Read slowly, taking plenty of pauses between sentences to allow the various images and sensations to be conjured in the imagination. If after you've recorded and listened to it, you feel that you've raced through it too fast, start again at a better pace:

Feel yourself getting drowsy, safe and relaxed. Your body is feeling heavy, your limbs feel limp and warm. The only sensation you are aware of is that of being breathed, breath rising and falling like gentle waves on a shore, in and out. You feel at peace. Relaxed. Warm. Heavy.

You are in a white empty place. You see a staircase in front of you. You go to the top of it and are looking down the stairs. They are going down and you start to go down them. One step at a time. One. As you go down you start to feel even more peaceful. Two. You can see the steps clearly going further down as you descend. Three. As you go deeper down it is getting quieter. Four. You feel even calmer as if each step down is taking you to a more restful place inside of yourself. Five steps. Silent. Six. You feel comfortable, safe and warm. Seven. Peaceful. Eight. Relaxed. Ninth step. By the time you get to the tenth step you'll be completely relaxed. As you get near to the bottom of the stairs you see a doorway in front of you. Light is flooding through this doorway, and warmth. White light and warmth. Ten.

You step off the stairway and go through the doorway. You find yourself in a beautiful garden. You can feel the soft rays and warmth of the sun and light in the garden. You walk right into the garden. It is abundant with flowers and shrubs in full bloom. The garden is fragrant with their scent. The air feels clean and fresh. The light is gentle. You feel safe and warm and relaxed. You look around at all the flowers and feel very happy. There is a small fountain and you can hear the gentle sound of running water. You can hear birds singing as you walk through this enchanting place. You can feel the soft grass under your feet.

Just beyond the garden you see some water and walk towards it. By the bank there is a small wooden boat which you climb into. The water is so still, gently lapping as you lie on soft cushions in the boat. The sun is shining down on you. You feel comfortable. Safe. At ease. You lie in the boat and it begins to lazily drift across the water. Gently rocking. You feel completely at peace in this safe, beautiful place under a blue, blue sky. You drift for a few minutes feeling very happy, content to hear the gentle lapping of the water and feel the sun's warm rays. You float in complete relaxation.

As you drift back in to the shore, you can see an open meadow. Scattered in the green grass are flowers. It is so green and lush and peaceful here. There is a wonderful feeling of open space. It is warm, with the sun still shining down warming you as you walk into it. You lie in the grass in the meadow. You can see trees in the distance and can smell the fresh scent of grass and clean air. As you lie in this place of tranquillity you feel completely relaxed, safe, warm, happy. Up above, the sky is clear blue. This is a wonderful place.

In a moment it will be time to go and you shall leave this place feeling very relaxed and calm. When you open your eyes you will feel refreshed and at peace with yourself. Your breathing is easy and comfortable and it is time to go. On the count of ten, you will awake feeling relaxed and refreshed. During the countdown, you will start to feel more and more awake. Ten, nine, starting to wake up now, eight, seven. Starting to feel refreshed and alert. Six, five, four, three, two, feeling wide awake, alert and revitalized. One. Open your eyes.

Stay a moment and enjoy the sensation of being relaxed and refreshed from your inner journey before getting up and starting to do things.

NB: Alternatively, you can make up a visualization tape with a scenario from your own imagination using favourite places and sensations that are particular to you as an individual.

Physical
Shortcuts

14

TAKE SEVERAL LONG, SLOW, DEEP BREATHS

TIME: *2 minutes, or longer if you wish*

INGREDIENTS: *none necessary*

METHOD

1   Inhale deeply right into the bottom of your lungs, feeling the abdomen swell as you inhale. Hold for a moment then exhale with a sigh, pushing the air out of your lungs as you do.

2   Repeat step one: inhale deeply, hold for a moment, let go with a sigh.

3   Breathe in slowly; this time exhale in your own time. The relaxing effect is immediate.

4   Continue taking deep breaths right into your abdomen for several moments.

This is one of the cheapest, simplest and most instant methods of calming down and you carry it around with you 24 hours a day. You can do it in traffic, at the office or in the middle of a row or tense situation without having to reach for any pill or potion and without having to adopt any posture or position that may not be appropriate for the situation. By its very nature, the breath is constant and life-giving, so it's no wonder that if we become aware of it we calm down.

Watch when people are under stress, depressed, angry or feeling over-emotional. You will see that their breathing becomes shallow: they breathe only to and from the top of the lungs.

When more relaxed, the breathing becomes deeper, slower and naturally uses the lower part of the lungs. By consciously slowing the breathing down and breathing deep into the bottom of the lungs and abdomen, you will find that your stress level will be reduced, and your concentration and performance will be improved.

15

A BREATHING TECHNIQUE TO SLOW AND CALM YOU

TIME: *5 minutes*

INGREDIENTS: *cushion to support your knees*

As a follow-up to the previous technique, this takes you a little deeper. It enhances the relaxing sensation of deep breathing by taking you into it in three stages.

METHOD

1 Lie down on your back with a cushion supporting your knees for maximum comfort. Gently rest your hands on the upper chest beneath the collar bone.

2 Breathe in slowly so that this part of the ribcage rises.

3 When you are ready, breathe out slowly so that all the air is expelled; then repeat the process. Let your hands be aware of the movement of the ribcage rising and falling as you repeat this process five to ten times.

4 This time, rest your hands on the lower ribcage. Again, breathe in slowly and, when you are ready, exhale until this part of the lungs is completely empty. Be aware of the rising and falling and how it feels in your lower ribcage as the lungs expand with inhalation and contract as you breathe out. Repeat the process slowly five to ten times.

5 Now rest your hands on your abdomen on either side of the navel. Breathe in slowly, right into this area, feeling the abdomen rising and pushing your hands up as you inhale, and the hands falling with the abdomen as you breathe out. Be aware of the air travelling through the upper lung to the lower lung and into the abdomen as you breathe in and out. Repeat the process five to ten times.

6 Get up slowly and resume your activities. You will find that you feel more serene in just a few moments by practising this simple technique.

Once you have practised the process through a few times, you will be able to apply it in any stressful situation for immediate results and relaxation.

16

IMPROVE POSTURE AND PREVENT FURTHER BACKACHE WITH THE HELP OF A SIMPLE VISUALIZATION

TIME: *2 minutes*

INGREDIENTS: *none necessary*

The technique below was told to me by a teacher of the Alexander method. It is a simple way of experiencing how it feels to have the spine in a stress-free position. The more often you remember to apply it, the more your body will start to recognize when it is slumped, slouching or twisting, and correct itself.

METHOD

1   Imagine that coming out of the top of your head is a cord to which is tied a helium balloon which is pulling you gently to the sky. At the base of the spine is a lead weight. Let your head lead you as you visualize these two opposite forces and, automatically, you will correct your posture. Your spine will lengthen and you'll find you sit or stand more upright.

You can practise it whenever you remember, for example, when you are slumped over your desk, whilst tense at the wheel of your car, or standing in a queue.

Once the spine and neck are free, the other organs of the body can rest more comfortably, the lungs aren't restricted and you can breathe more deeply. If you're slouched over, the lungs are compressed, you don't get enough oxygen and so can't function as well as you should.

The Alexander technique is fast becoming a popular alternative therapy. It was formulated almost 100 years ago by an actor called Frederick

Alexander. The idea behind his technique is to make a person aware of their posture and of any bad habits that they may have fallen into while sitting, standing or working, as it is these that cause back strain and tension to build. Alexander believed that it is only when we are aware of the incorrect posture that we can we begin to change it.

The technique teaches ways to bring the body back into correct alignment by showing positions in which there is minimum strain on the skeleton. It allows you to use the back more naturally and thus avoid problems before they arise. It helps unlearn bad habits that sometimes have been with us since childhood and which, if perpetuated, can lead to back strain, backache, round shoulders and, in some cases, the badly curved spines you can see in some elderly people.

The Alexander method aims to re-educate the body through gentle manual guidance and verbal instruction. New habits are learnt which will correct the old habits that we may have unconsciously fallen into. By restoring the body's natural reflexes, the technique undoes some of the uncomfortable muscular distortions that we can get ourselves into daily whilst sitting, standing, lifting or driving.

Alexander instructors aim to help make people conscious of how they are incorrectly holding themselves. The way they do this is by demonstrating how it feels to hold oneself correctly. As soon as the body experiences this for itself and becomes aware of the difference, it can start to correct itself.

Just a few lessons with an Alexander teacher can improve a lifetime's bad posture, improve relaxation, reduce stress levels and reduce the number of appointments required with osteopaths etc. The teacher can also show you how to adapt your posture according to your job requirements. Anyone in a job that involves bending over for prolonged periods of times – whether a nurse, dentist, mechanic or someone working at a desk all day – knows how this can adversely affect the lower back.

When I started out working as an aromatherapist, by the end of each day I had chronic lower back pain as a result of bending over my couch working on clients. I had six lessons with an Alexander teacher who taught me how to shift my weight and posture according to what I was doing. After months of debilitating backache, I haven't had a problem since and that was over 10 years ago. It proved to be a worthwhile investment.

For further information on how to contact a teacher in your area, turn to the back of the book to the Useful Addresses section.

17

SIT CORRECTLY TO MINIMIZE BACK STRAIN

TIME: *as often as you remember*

INGREDIENTS: *chair*

Only too often when people sit down, they slump, sag, slouch and cross their arms and legs, twisting themselves into positions which temporarily may appear to be the most comfortable but can ultimately strain the back or neck and build up stress in these areas. Crossing your legs will twist the pelvis and spine. Slouching can restrict your breathing.

The Alexander technique guides people to a correct position for sitting in which the spine is in its most natural position and so can be maintained like this for a long period of time without aching. This is particularly useful in situations where you are stuck in one sitting position for a long time and can't move too much, for example, on an aeroplane, driving in a car, at your desk, or in the small spaces at theatres and some cinemas.

METHOD

1 When you sit, use the image mentioned previously – that a cord is coming out of the top of the head gently pulling the head skywards. This automatically lifts the neck and lengthens and straightens the spine.

2 As you go to sit, don't stiffen your neck. Keep your neck and spine in alignment and imagine that you are going to squat. Now bend the knees and hips while at the same time letting your head go forward and up. Feel the spine lengthen and widen. As you bend your knees to go into a sitting position, allow your weight to go onto the sitting bone. Also as you bend, keep your feet parallel. Your knees should be open slightly and will naturally go forward and away.

3 When sitting, keep slightly forward with your weight on the front part of the pelvic bones, resisting the urge to slump back arching your lower back. Keep shoulders relaxed, knees a little apart and your feet firmly on the floor.

This position can be maintained comfortably for a considerable amount of time.

4 When you need to get up, imagine coming up from a squat again. Let the head lead you and feel the spine lengthen and widen as you stand up.

If you try this, you can feel how it minimizes strain on the back, and if you practise a few times daily, it will soon become automatic.

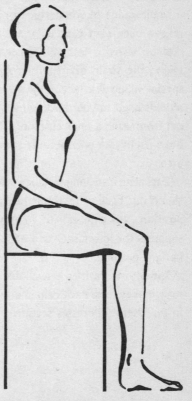

Incorrect posture for sitting   Correct posture for sitting

18

BACK SUPPORT FOR THE CAR

TIME: *for use every time you drive*

INGREDIENTS: *Sitting Partner cushion*

If you're someone who suffers from lower back pain every time you drive, especially long distances, you will benefit from support for your lower back.

The best support I have come across in my research is available from the British School of Osteopathy's shop (called Back in Action), where they sell a whole range of wonderful furniture and gadgets specially designed to relieve back pain caused by sitting awkwardly. It is a small adjustable cushion called a Sitting Partner, which shapes and supports the spine, taking the strain off painful ligaments, muscles and discs. It also has a special filling that keeps the lower back warm. The cushion adapts and moulds itself to your back, preventing the uncomfortable feeling you can get from using a small cushion: after a while, it can often seem like you've got a fist in your back because the cushion presses too hard into the lumbar area.

Backache from long distance driving can be a result of bad posture, as we slump our back or arch our neck trying to get into a more comfortable position. This pain can be improved by the Sitting Partner as it gently supports the lower back and helps the spine maintain a more natural and upright position.

The Sitting Partner is available by mail order and each one sold helps raise money for a Back Pain charity. The address for Back in Action is given in the Useful Addresses section.

19

A QUICK STRETCH FOR RELEASING BACK AND NECK TENSION

TIME: *2–5 minutes*

INGREDIENTS: *a clear wall*

This process loosens tight muscles and can be done anywhere and anytime for fast relief for a strained back and shoulders.

METHOD

1   Find a clear wall with room for your arms to be raised on either side without obstruction.

2   Stand with your back against the wall. Ensure that you can feel the wall with the back of your head, your shoulders and your buttocks.

3   Inhale deeply, right into your abdomen. At the same time lift your arms outwards up to shoulder height, hands turned so that the palms are facing out to the front (this opens up the chest area). Hold this position for a few moments then lower your arms. Repeat three to four times.

4   Now come away from the wall and lie on the floor with your arms up over your head.

5   With your right arm and right foot reach away from the mid-line around your waist. Stretch as far as you can with your arm and your foot in opposite directions. Hold for a few moments, then relax and repeat on the left side.

6   Repeat on both sides five to ten times.

7   To get up, roll on your side, bend your knees and come up slowly.

20

A PROCESS TO RELIEVE LOWER BACK PAIN

TIME: *5–10 minutes*

INGREDIENTS: *none necessary*

METHOD

1 Lie on the floor on your back with your arms out at shoulder level.

2 Bring your knees up so that they are bent, feet on the floor. Let your feet come up as you take your knees over to the left. At the same time, take both arms over to the right at shoulder level.

3 Repeat to the other side.

4 To enhance the stretch and increase leverage, as you take your legs to the left and arms to the right, first of all bend your knees, feet flat on the floor, and cross your left leg over your right. Now take your legs over to the left. For the other side, again bend your knees, feet flat on the floor, and cross your right leg over your left leg. Take your legs over to the right while your arms go to the left.

You will find this gives even more relief to the lower back.

5 Repeat five to ten times.

6 Still lying on your back, bring your knees up towards your chest, feet off the floor.

7 Put your hands behind your knees and gently pull them towards you. You will feel this gently stretching the lower back and relieving any tightness there.

21

A GENTLE ROTATION TO RELIEVE TENSION IN THE SPINE

TIME: *5–10 minutes*

INGREDIENTS: *chair, small cushion, belt or long scarf*

This easy process can relieve stiffness and tension caused from either working at a desk for a prolonged period of time or doing an activity where you have been bent over straining your back.

METHOD

1 Sit comfortably but up straight and tall with your feet parallel on the floor, your knees slightly apart. It is essential that you don't slouch for this.

2 Place one hand on your right wrist, the other coming under your left wrist. Bring your arms up in front of you, level with your shoulders and about eight inches away from your chest.

3 Take your folded arms to the left and turn your head at the same time as though looking to your left side. Hold at the end of this rotation for a few moments and keep breathing normally through-out. Come back to the middle.

4 Repeat to the right, again holding for a few moments at the end of the rotation.

Rather than wait until your back has seized up, stop and do this gentle rotation every now and then to help prevent a build-up of tension in the spine.

5 Next, kneel on a folded blanket or towel with your knees together and sit on your heels. (If this is difficult put a small cushion under your buttocks.) Interlock your fingers, breathe out and stretch your arms above your head turning your palms upwards. Take a few breaths in this position, then bring your arms down.

6 Take your hands behind your back, and link your fingers, palms away from you. Sitting up straight, let your shoulders relax and push your hands away from your lower back. Hold this position for a few moments, breathing normally.

7 Stretch your legs out in front of you with your weight a little to the front of your buttocks so that you can lift your lower back. Stretch up and forwards and reach slowly towards your feet. If this is difficult then loop a scarf or belt around your feet and hold onto that instead. Keep your legs straight and move from the base of your spine, not just the upper back. Keep the shoulders relaxed and elongate the back of the neck. Hold this position for 30 seconds, breathing normally. Take a few deep breaths, then, when you are ready, bend your knees, get up slowly and resume your activities.

NB: Do not attempt this if suffering from a serious back or neck problem.

22

A RELAXATION PROCESS FOR NECK AND SHOULDERS

TIME: *5–10 minutes*

INGREDIENTS: *none necessary*

This process is useful when you're feeling the strain in neck and shoulder muscles. Just putting five minutes aside to run through it can alleviate aches and restore vitality.

METHOD

1 Stand up straight with your feet slightly apart. Inhale and slowly lift both shoulders up towards your ears. Hold this position for a few moments.

2 Exhale and lower the shoulders to their normal position.

3 Repeat this five times.

4 Rotate your left shoulder backwards (i.e. up, back, down, in and back to normal). Repeat this with the right shoulder.

5 Do this five times on each side.

6 Rotate the left shoulder forwards (i.e. up, forward, down, in and back to normal). Repeat this with the right shoulder.

7 Do this five times on both sides.

8 Now let your neck relax, let the head come forward until your chin rests on your chest. Slowly return to upright.

10 Repeat five times.

11 Pull your shoulder blades back as though trying to make them meet. Hold for a few moments then return to normal.

12 Slowly and without straining, let your head tilt towards your left shoulder. Return to upright. Repeat tilting to the right shoulder.

13 Repeat five times.

14 Next let your head roll very slowly, starting by letting it drop forward on to the chest, then roll towards the right shoulder. Hold for a few moments then roll back to the centre again. Repeat to the other side.

15 Repeat five times.

NB: Never strain or force the neck if it doesn't want to go. On step 14, don't be tempted to roll the head back from the shoulder at any point as this can strain the spine.

23

HANG UPSIDE DOWN IN A PAIR OF GRAVITY BOOTS!

TIME: *as long as feels comfortable*

INGREDIENTS: *gravity boots, sturdy door frame*

Great for those who like their relaxation techniques to be different!

Gravity boots can be purchased from any major sports equipment shop. They are a sturdy pair of boots that come with a suspension bar which is screwed securely into the top of a door frame. Once in place, you secure the boots to the ankles with hooks in front and latches on the outside of the legs, swing up and into position and hang upside down by your ankles which allows gravity to stretch and relax the whole body. Hanging like this allows your body weight to traction the spine, decompressing the joints and discs.

The benefits are claimed to be improved back and joint aches, improved posture, decompressed discs and joints, improved circulation, increased flexibility of the spine and joints and generally relief of stress and tension.

Many scientists say that the force of gravity is a major factor in vertebral misalignments. These misalignments along the vertebral joints, together with the narrowing of a compressed disc, put pressure on the spinal nerves existing between them. This pressure is the cause of many health problems and back pain.

NB: This is not a method to be recommended for anyone with serious health problems, heart trouble or serious weight problems. Otherwise, it certainly gives you the chance to look at life from another angle!

Most gravity boots also come with a set of exercise instructions that you can also do with the bar and boots.

CAUTION

Those who are pregnant or suffering from high blood pressure, heart disease, obesity or a serious health condition should consult their doctor before use.

24

SALUTATIONS TO THE SUN

TIME: *5–10 minutes*

INGREDIENTS: *none necessary*

This sequence of body-toning yoga exercises is an excellent way to start the day. It synchronizes breathing with stretching and will help shake off any stiffness or tension. Study the sequence and practise before doing it properly. As it becomes part of your routine, you won't need the diagram.

Don't force the movements; they are meant to be carried out smoothly and easily. Recognize your own limitations and don't hurry through them. Do them slowly. Depending on your fitness level you can do the sequence once, twice or three times. (Don't feel you have to do it more than once as even one run-through will be of benefit.)

METHOD

The sequence:

1. Knees/feet/palms together

2. Breathe in gently and bend backwards, palms up

3. Breathe out and bend forward

4. Breathe in, put palms flat on floor and look up

5. Hold breath, both legs back

6. Breathe out, rest buttocks on heels and put forehead on floor

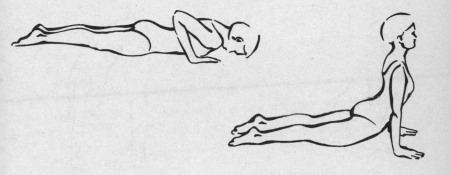

7. Breathe in, then out. Take weight on hands then rest forehead and chest on floor

8. Breathe in, straighten arms, arch back and stretch head up

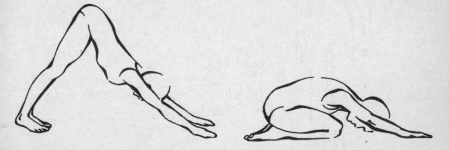

9. Breathe out, buttocks up, hands and feet flat on floor

10. Breathe in, then out. Rest buttocks on heels and forehead on floor

11. Breathe in and stretch forwards with hands flat on floor

12. Breathe out with straight legs and bend from the waist

13. Breathe in and stand up

25

TAKE REGULAR EXERCISE

TIME: *20 minutes, four times a week*

INGREDIENTS: *variable on your choice*

Choose an exercise that you take pleasure in and make it a priority booking in your diary.

I'm not going to specify a particular exercise here as I believe one of the main ingredients in exercising is that you enjoy it, otherwise you'll only keep it up for the first few weeks then drop it.

On the next page is a list to give you an idea of all the various forms of exercise on offer these days. Some are strenuous, others are gentler, but there's bound to be something within the bounds of possibility for everyone of all ages and abilities.

Exercise can transform the level of mental and physical health dramatically, producing a sense of well-being almost instantly, so it is obviously going to benefit anyone who is under stress and needs to feel more relaxed. Physical activity has long been recognized for its uplifting effect on dull or depressed states of mind. As feeling physically dull can result in feeling mentally and emotionally dull, exercise is an obvious advantage.

All the physiological processes of the body will improve, as exercise stimulates all the vital organs. The more physically fit you are, the better you will perform on every level. Circulation is stimulated, reducing the presence of lactic acid which can result in shallow breathing and a feeling of lethargy.

The hormone epinephrine (adrenaline) is produced in large quantities after only a short time. This is the hormone that results in the common feeling of well-being, or 'high', that many people speak of experiencing after exercise.

Just 20 minutes four times a week can change your state of mind as well as fitness levels. You'll feel better for making the effort.

TYPES OF EXERCISE

A – aerobics

B – badminton, basketball, bowling, ballet

C – cricket, cycling, canoeing,

D – dancing, diving,

E – Egyptian dancing

F – football, fencing

G – gym, golf

H – horse riding, hockey

J – jogging, judo, jazz classes

K – kick boxing

L – line dancing

M – Morris dancing

N – netball

P – private trainers for home exercise, Pilates exercises

R – rugby, running, rowing, rounders, rollerskating, rollerblading

S – step classes, swimming, squash, skating

T – Tai Chi, tennis, table tennis

V – videos for home use (with the wide range of excellent exercise videos available nowadays, you can always exercise at home on those days when you haven't time to get out)

W – walking, wrestling, weight training, wind surfing

Y – yoga

26

A COMFORTABLE POSITION TO RELIEVE LOWER BACK, LEG OR FOOT ACHE

TIME: *5–10 minutes*

INGREDIENTS: *chair, towel*

This is a relaxing position to lie in for a few minutes if you have been on your feet for hours or working at a desk or computer all day and your lower back, feet or legs are aching and tired.

METHOD

1 Change into comfortable unrestricted clothing.

2 Place a chair against a wall.

3 Put a towel or folded blanket on the floor and lie down on your back.

4 Bend your knees and put your feet up on the chair and simply lie like this for as long as you feel like. For added relief, you may want to put two average size books under your head to help support the neck.

5 For enhanced relaxation of the back, roll a towel and place it beneath the spine.

Most of the time during the day, whether standing or sitting, unless we have perfect posture, our lower back is under strain as we either arch or slump. In this position, your lower back is completely flat against the floor and so supported and comfortable. This position is also good for swollen and aching legs.

While lying in this position, you could increase your relaxation by listening to a piece of tranquil music or one of the many relaxation tapes now available. See the address of a supplier at the back of the book in the Useful Addresses section.

27

LIE IN THE ALEXANDER POSITION FOR RELAXATION

TIME: *15–20 minutes*

INGREDIENTS: *two or three books of average thickness*

The Alexander position for relaxation is an excellent way to gently undo strain and tension held in the spine and neck.

METHOD

Simply lie down on your back on the floor in the position shown in the diagram, with two or three books (average paperbacks will be thick enough) beneath your head so that it is comfortably supported.

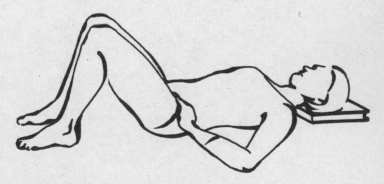

Hands rest gently on your hip-bones, knees bent. Your elbows are out at an angle on the floor, your knees slightly apart, parallel with your hips

Stay like this for 20 minutes, or more if you feel like it.

In this position, the head and neck are supported by the books, the legs are bent, so removing any strain from the lower back, and the spine lies comfortably flat along the floor. This gives the spine a chance to realign itself and ease out any tension that has built up because of bad posture or stress during the day.

People find that in this position their breathing becomes more relaxed and they have renewed energy when they get up; they also become aware of how stiffly they have been previously holding themselves. All you have to do is lie down as shown and relax. What could be easier?

28

LIE ON A BACKSTRETCHER FOR MUSCLE RELEASE AND RELAXATION

TIME: *10 minutes, or as long as feels comfortable*

INGREDIENTS: *backstretcher, small cushion*

Lying for 10 minutes on this specially formulated backstretcher is equivalent to a 10-minute shiatsu massage and can relieve stress, backache, muscle strain and poor posture. It was awarded the best new healthcare and medical product of 1995.

The backstretcher is a curved wooden contraption about the size of an average back and looks a bit like an old-fashioned washing board. It has thumb-like nodules that make contact either side of the spine when you lie back, while the spine itself lies suspended above a channel between the nodules so that it doesn't come into contact with the wood at all. The curved shape of the wood gently stretches the back as you relax onto it.

METHOD

1 Put the backstretcher on the floor and sit down about six inches away.

2 Align the spine with the central channel then lie back slowly, using a cushion behind the head for support and comfort.

3 When in position, bend your knees to take pressure from the lower back.

4 As you relax you can move back along it, letting the arch-shape gently stretch the back and the nodules massage the points along the sides of the spine.

5 Lie in position for up to 10 minutes.

6   To get up, slowly slide back to your starting position, roll sideways and gently sit up.

NB: It is not recommended for pregnant women or anyone with brittle bones or fused vertebrae.

Backstretchers can be bought by mail order and are available from the address at the back in the Useful Addresses section.

29

HAVE MUSCLE TENSION MASSAGED AWAY IN A HYDROTHERAPY BATH

TIME: *as long as you like*

INGREDIENTS: *hydrotherapy bath*

I recently came across a wonderful invention at the Olympia Health fair in London: a hydrotherapy bath with a difference. It is portable so you can take it with you when you move house or even take it away with you if travelling for a few weeks.

Once upon a time the only place you could get a good hydrotherapy bath was at a health farm or clinic, but this one is available so that you can enjoy the benefits in the comfort of your own home. And it doesn't require any plumbing in. It is a lightweight portable system that comes with a small pump and a unit that fits into any average bath. You put it in and take it out as required, which means it is also easily accessible for cleaning.

If you have a bit of spare cash, it's the perfect addition to any anti-stress programme and could be invaluable if you regularly suffer from backache and tension. It gives a deep, relaxing water massage through thousands of small jets streaming out bubbles. The combination of warm water and the massage from the jets is a wonderful way to end the day, especially if it's been a day that's put a strain on back and neck muscles, or left you feeling generally stressed.

The bath has: 1,000 tiny jets which gently soothe the back and neck and improve circulation; 800 medium jets which work on the larger muscles of the back, shoulder and neck, stimulating deeper tissue and giving a more vigorous massage, which is good for muscular pain, stiff joints, general stress and tension; 200 large jets which move with more force and will give a sensation of being pummelled by the water. These large jets are positioned so that they concentrate on either side of the spine.

There is a choice of 50 combinations of massage, of varying lengths and degrees of intensity, so you can suit your changing requirements. The control heel is at the bottom of the unit, so you don't even need to get up to change the controls.

To heighten the wonderful sensation of massage with warm water, you could add four to six drops of essential oil. Depending on personal preference, you can choose from lavender, camomile, rosewood, marjoram, sandalwood, ylang ylang, rose or neroli, all of which will help the relaxation process.

Some stockists of these baths are given in the Useful Addresses section.

30

AN EXERCISE TO RELAX AND REFRESH THE EYES

TIME: *5 minutes*

INGREDIENTS: *chair/table*

This exercise will rest and strengthen the eyes if strained from computer work, reading, driving or long periods of concentration.

Steps four to seven involve some visualization to be done with closed eyes, so either read these steps through a few times so that you remember what to do or, alternatively, ask a friend or relative to read these steps out to you as you go through the process. After a few times, it will become familiar and you will be able to remember it.

METHOD

1 Start by shifting your point of focus. Often eyes become tired through staring at one small area for a prolonged period of time. Stare into the distance. Then to the left, to the right. Have a good look around, resting your eyes on various objects at different distances away from whatever you've been working on.

2 Let your shoulders drop if you're hunched up, and sit up straight.

3 Close your eyes tightly for a few moments.

4 Rest your elbows on your desk or table and lightly cover both eyes completely with the palms of your hands. Take a few long deep breaths right into your abdomen then rest in the darkness for a few moments.

5 Keep your eyes covered and your breathing deep. As you inhale, imagine energy from the breath going into the eye area. Do this a few times.

6 With eyes still closed, imagine that you are looking a long way off to some distant horizon, far over the sea or fields or up into blue skies or a starry night.

7 Now imagine you are at the sea watching the waves come in and go out. They come in as you inhale, go out as you exhale. Stay with this image, matching it with your breathing for a few minutes.

8 Now uncover your eyes and using the thumb and the index finger from both hands, press along the bony ridge below and above the eyes.

9 Pinch the bridge of the nose with the thumb and index finger then, starting on the inside of the eyebrow (again with thumb and index finger), pinch along the eyebrow. Hold each pinch for a few seconds then release. (This brings blood and oxygen to the eye area.)

10 Repeat step nine if you want to. Then take a deep breath and resume work looking up every now and again to shift your point of focus and prevent further eye strain.

Nutritional Shortcuts

31

EAT A BALANCED NUTRITIOUS DIET FOR A SOUND MIND AND BODY

TIME: *just however long it takes to choose when food-shopping*

'You are what you eat' may be a cliché but the fact is that our basic diet has a tremendous effect, not only on how we look, but also on how we feel. If you've been experiencing fatigue, stress or agitation, it can be remedied by altering your dietary habits. If you eat rubbish, you can often end up feeling that way. If you're not getting the proper nutrients from your food, you're not going to have the energy you need to function to your maximum potential and can often feel like you're 'running on empty'.

However, if you eat plenty of fresh fruit and vegetables and nutritious food, you'll feel more vibrant, look better and have more energy. This needn't be a great headache that involves cooking complicated meals and following difficult rules. Just simply bear in mind the following principles when shopping for food and you'll be on your way to better health and energy levels.

These are the basic rudiments for a balanced diet.

Plenty of fresh fruit and fresh vegetables

Fruit and vegetables are high in vitamins and minerals plus they contain fibre and plenty of water. The fibre content of these foods helps prevent constipation. The following tips should help keep the vitamin content in food:

- Eat fruit and vegetables without cooking whenever you can, e.g. raw vegetables in salads, fresh fruit.
- Cook frozen vegetables straight from the freezer without thawing. (Frozen vegetables retain more nutrients than canned ones.)

- Microwave/stir fry or steam vegetables whenever possible, or add vegetables to already boiling water as this reduces the cooking time.

Whole grain cereals, bread, brown rice, barley, millet, pulses

Small amounts of fish and lean meats

Fish contains high levels of essential fatty acids that protect against heart disease, high cholesterol levels and other degenerative diseases.

Diets high in red meat have been linked with degenerative diseases of the gut, and their fat content is frequently too high.

Small amounts of low-fat dairy products and yoghurt

Avoidance where possible of refined foods, prepacked foods, foods containing additives, caffeine, strong condiments

Refined foods have been stripped of much of their goodness; prolonged use may result in a vitamin and mineral deficiency. Also, many refined and processed foods contain a combination of artificial additives which don't do any good to overall health.

Reduce sugar and sugar products

Sugar products supply the body with an excess of instant energy which can lead to excessive fluctuations in blood glucose levels. This may result in periods of low energy and mood swings; also, sugar doesn't contain any nutrients.

Reduce your salt intake

A lot of salt in the diet is linked with high blood pressure (which can lead to heart disease). It also impairs mineral utilization in the body.

Keep alcohol consumption to a moderate level

Alcohol is high in calories so can easily lead to weight gain; excessive alcohol drinking can damage the liver.

Use cold-pressed virgin oils

Drink plenty of water

32

ENSURE THAT YOU'RE GETTING ENOUGH OF THE B VITAMINS IN YOUR DIET

TIME: *just as long as it takes to swallow*

INGREDIENTS: *foods rich in B vitamins, as stated below, or a B complex supplement*

A good intake of the B vitamins will contribute to having a healthy nervous system and balanced state of mind. Vitamin B is often recommended when under stress, as a prolonged lack of it can lead to a downward spiral: when under stress, the body uses up its vitamin B supply, and a lack of it can lead to fatigue, depression, anxiety, high blood pressure – more stress. Continued tension robs us of essential nutrients and slows down digestion, as well as weakening resistance to disease, so it is important to ensure that there is a daily intake of the B vitamins, either through diet or supplements.

The chances are that if your diet is a good, well-balanced one (see shortcut 31), then you should be getting an adequate supply of the B vitamins through your food. But if you have been in a prolonged stressful situation living on a diet of coffee, fast foods and takeaways, you may be deficient. The B vitamins are water-soluble and any excess is excreted and not stored in the body, so it is important to top up levels daily.

People who smoke, drink a lot of alcohol or are vegetarian particularly need to ensure that they are getting adequate amounts.

POSSIBLE RESULTS OF B VITAMIN DEFICIENCIES

B1: loss of appetite, lack of concentration, weakness, fatigue, constipation, nausea, shortness of breath, irritability, depression.
B2: cracks and sores in the corner of the mouth, inflammation of the tongue, insomnia, conjunctivitis, dermatitis, trembling.
B3: fatigue, lack of appetite, ulcers, depression, insomnia, irritability.

B5: cramp, asthma, fatigue, insomnia, susceptibility to allergies.

B6: anaemia, dermatitis.

B9: fatigue, weakness, irritability, insomnia, confusion, shortness of breath, anaemia.

B12: anaemia, loss of appetite, irritability, degeneration of the nervous system.

Biotin: nerve disorders.

Go into any health shop and ask what they recommend for stress and the chances are that they'll point you to the shelf where the vitamin B complex is. Although these supplements can help in temporary situations to support efforts to stay in good health, they shouldn't be taken as an easy alternative to a good diet. The general feeling from most nutritionists is that it is best to try and alter your diet and use nature's supplements by ensuring that you are getting the daily nutrients you need from your food.

NATURAL SOURCES

The B vitamins are present in the following foods: Brewer's yeast, whole wheat, milk, meat, liver, leafy green vegetables, fish, eggs, kidney, cheese, whole brown rice, pumpkin seeds, apricots, peaches, seafood, pulses, soya beans.

For a quick natural boost of B vitamin-rich food, eat either a handful of pumpkin seeds or dried apricots, a few slices of wholemeal bread or a bowl of fortified breakfast cereal with a banana before you start out in the morning.

NB: If in any doubt as to how much vitamin B to take as a supplement (or how much to take of any of the vitamins and minerals that are recommended in the following section), consult a nutritionist. Dosages can vary depending on an individual's circumstances, lifestyle and diet and on any other supplements they may be taking at the time.

Many nutritionists advise not to take large doses of individual vitamins over prolonged periods without professional guidance because the complicated synergism of vitamin and mineral absorption is a science in itself and can be thrown out of balance if one is taken in isolation. If we eat properly we should get sufficient amounts for good health. Sadly, however, much of the nutrient content in food is lost through canning, freezing, preserving, shipping and storage of food, which is why supplementation is sometimes necessary.

An address for a supplier of good quality supplements is given at the back of the book in the Useful Addresses section.

33

ENSURE THAT YOU'RE GETTING ENOUGH VITAMIN C IN YOUR DIET

TIME: *just as long as it takes to swallow*

INGREDIENTS: *foods rich in vitamin C, as stated below, or a vitamin C supplement*

The body's vitamin C level can get depleted when under stress, particularly if you are a heavy drinker or smoker. (The minimum daily requirement for vitamin C is 30mg [milligrams]. One cigarette uses up 25mg.)

As vitamin C is necessary for good health and energy, it is important to ensure that you are getting enough in your diet. Vitamin C helps fight infection, protects substances in the body from oxidizing, improves adrenal hormone output and helps to normalize blood sugar metabolism. As it is water-soluble (like the B vitamins), it is also excreted from the body after two to three hours so it is important to keep levels up, either through natural food sources or with supplements (see note about supplements at the end of shortcut 32).

POSSIBLE RESULTS OF VITAMIN C DEFICIENCY

Fatigue, irritability, weakness, tender joints, bleeding and soft gums, anaemia, slow wound healing and, in severe cases, scurvy.

NATURAL SOURCES

Vitamin C is present in citrus fruits, rosehips, blackcurrants, tomatoes, milk, leafy green vegetables, potatoes, strawberries.

For a quick, natural boost of vitamin C have a glass of freshly squeezed orange juice in the morning (one orange contains approximately 60mg of vitamin C), half a grapefruit or a helping of broccoli with a meal (an average helping contains 34mg).

As a supplement, it can be taken in tablet form or in syrups, powders or pastilles.

34

ENSURE THAT YOU'RE GETTING ENOUGH VITAMIN E IN YOUR DIET

TIME: *just as long as it takes to swallow*

INGREDIENTS: *foods rich in vitamin E, as stated below, or a vitamin E supplement*

Fatigue, high blood pressure, chest pains, anaemia, loss of sex drive, dry skin and early ageing are all common signs of stress. They are also symptoms that can occur when there is a vitamin E deficiency, so if any of the above sound familiar, the chances are you will benefit from either introducing more foods rich in vitamin E or taking a vitamin E supplement (see note about supplements at the end of shortcut 32). Vitamin E is also good for heart conditions and can help act as a preventative if sufficient is taken, either through foods rich in vitamin E or through supplements.

One of the functions of vitamin E is to improve the oxygenation of cells. As one of the antioxidant family, it helps to counteract any damage done by pollution, unsaturated fats and sunshine.

POSSIBLE RESULTS OF VITAMIN E DEFICIENCY

Muscle weakness, dull hair and skin.

NATURAL SOURCES

Vitamin E is found in wheat germ, soya, vegetable oils, nuts and seeds, broccoli, green vegetables, eggs and wholewheat cereals.

For a quick, natural boost to your daily diet, have a handful of peanuts, pumpkin or sunflower seeds, a glass of milk or an egg.

As a supplement, it is available in oil-based capsules and water-soluble dry-based tablets.

35

ENSURE THAT YOU'RE GETTING ADEQUATE MAGNESIUM IN YOUR DIET

TIME: *just as long as it takes to swallow*

INGREDIENTS: *foods rich in magnesium, as stated below, or a magnesium supplement*

If vitamin B is known as the anti-stress vitamin, so magnesium is known as the anti-stress mineral because it is essential for effective nerve functioning and can help in fighting depression.

As with vitamin B and C, many people who consume large amounts of alcohol are often magnesium-deficient.

POSSIBLE RESULTS OF MAGNESIUM DEFICIENCY

Weakness, nausea, anxiety, cramps, loss of appetite, PMT, insomnia, irregular or rapid heartbeat.

NATURAL SOURCES

Magnesium is found in milk, eggs, lemons, grapefruits, apples, seeds, almonds, dark green vegetables, yellow corn, whole grains, nuts (especially peanuts) and shellfish.

The recommended daily requirement is around 300mg. For a quick natural boost, have a jacket potato (50mg), or a bowl of muesli (50mg), a few slices of wholemeal bread or a handful of almonds or seeds.

Magnesium can also be found in dolomite (a natural supplement which also contains calcium) and is often recommended in this form. It is also usually present in ready-made multi-vitamin and mineral tablets (see note about supplements at the end of shortcut 32).

36

ENSURE THAT YOU'RE GETTING ENOUGH ZINC IN YOUR DIET

TIME: *just as long as it takes to swallow*

INGREDIENTS: *foods rich in zinc, as stated below, or a zinc supplement*

Zinc is essential for good health, skin and nervous tissues. It promotes growth, alertness and healthy development, speeds up wound healing and contractability of muscle, and is necessary for the release of insulin and the normal functioning of many enzymes. It also affects stress levels because it is necessary for the production of adrenal hormones. As it is used up quickly if under stress, it is important that levels aren't depleted.

POSSIBLE RESULTS OF ZINC DEFICIENCY

White spots under the nails, brittle nails, depression, irritability, impotence, lack of taste, smell and appetite, slow healing of wounds and a weak immune system.

There are only small levels of zinc in the average diet due to food refining and processing, pollution, and soil low in nutrients. It is also depleted by alcohol, smoking and excessive sugar intake.

NATURAL SOURCES

Zinc is found in fish and shellfish (particularly herrings and oysters), liver, red meat, whole grains, peas, yeast, nuts, wheat germ, pumpkin and sesame seeds and eggs.

For a quick natural boost have a couple of eggs on a few slices of wholemeal bread, or sprinkle sesame and pumpkin seeds on your vegetables.

37

ENSURE THAT YOU'RE GETTING ADEQUATE CALCIUM IN YOUR DIET

TIME: *just as long as it takes to swallow*

INGREDIENTS: *foods rich in calcium, as stated below, or a calcium supplement*

Calcium is also necessary in the fight against stress as it aids the nervous system and can help alleviate insomnia. It is the most abundant mineral present in the body; 99 per cent of it is for healthy bones and teeth but the remaining 1 per cent helps maintain a healthy nervous system, blood clotting, heart and enzyme reactions.

POSSIBLE RESULTS OF CALCIUM DEFICIENCY

Osteoporosis, rickets, cramps, irritability. It can also be a contributory factor in arthritic conditions.

NATURAL SOURCES

Calcium is found in dairy products, cheese, milk (which is why a milk drink last thing at night is often taken to calm the nerves), yoghurt, watercress, sesame seeds, soya beans, sunflower seeds, peanuts, walnuts, fish (especially sardines and salmon), broccoli and dried peas and beans.

For a quick, natural boost to your diet, have an ounce of hard cheese (28g), or half a pint of milk (284ml), a few slices of wholemeal bread or sprinkle a handful of sesame and sunflower seeds over your meal.

38

ENSURE A HEALTHY INTAKE OF SELENIUM

TIME: *just as long as it takes to swallow*

INGREDIENTS: *foods rich in selenium, as stated below, or selenium capsules*

Selenium is a trace mineral that works as an antioxidant, which means that it will help to slow down the ageing process (often accelerated by stress) as well as the hardening of tissue through oxidation. It also promotes a healthy old age and protects the arteries by destroying the toxins in the blood which can damage artery walls.

POSSIBLE RESULTS OF SELENIUM DEFICIENCY

Premature loss of stamina, liver problems, arthritis and skin problems. Low selenium soil has been associated with an increased risk of cancer and there are many doctors who will argue that selenium can help in the prevention of the disease.

NATURAL SOURCES

Selenium is found in liver, kidney, garlic, seafoods (especially tuna), egg yolk, Brewer's yeast, bran, wheat germ, onions and broccoli – although with grains and vegetables the selenium content will depend upon the soil in which they were grown.

The amount of selenium needed for good health is very small, not more than 0.2mg per day. For a quick natural boost, you should get sufficient from having a couple of eggs, a portion of broccoli or a bowl of cereal with bran and wheat germ.

39

TAKE GINSENG FOR FATIGUE AND DEPRESSION

TIME: *just as long as it takes to swallow*

INGREDIENTS: *ginseng capsules, tea, powder or tonic*

Ginseng is an excellent aid in times of stress crisis as it can increase stamina and vitality both mentally and physically. As well as being an all-round tonic, it also acts as an anti-depressant and a mild laxative, and helps with high and low blood pressure, insomnia, exhaustion, and poor circulation. In addition, it helps assimilate vitamins and minerals by acting as an endocrine stimulant.

It has been used in the East, particularly in China and Korea, for over 5,000 years as a tonic and energy stimulant. It is now available from most health shops and chemists and can be bought in capsule form or as tea, liquid concentrate, powder or root.

NB: Ginseng is most effective if taken on an empty stomach.

40

TAKE KAL. PHOS TO SOOTHE NERVES AND RELIEVE TENSION

TIME: *just as long as it takes to swallow*

INGREDIENTS: *kal. phos tablets*

Kal. phosphate (potassium phosphate) is one of 12 biochemic tissue salts and is used as a remedy for tension, poor memory, headaches, depression, indigestion, insomnia, nervous exhaustion and irritability due to worry.

Biochemics was developed in the 1870s by Dr Wilhelm Schuessler who worked at the time as a homoeopathic doctor. He named 12 tissue salts as being vital for good health and believed that an imbalance or lack of any of these essential tissue salts could cause a range of illnesses and symptoms.

Tissue salts are inorganic mineral components of the body tissue and a correct balance of all the natural mineral salts is essential for the healthy functioning of bodily cells, and overall good health. Kal. phosphate is found in all tissue parts, the nerves, the brain and blood cells. An imbalance or lack of any of the salts can cause illness and, in the case of a lack of kal. phosphate, all the symptoms listed above. Taking tissue salts can redress any imbalance, restore health and allow the body to heal itself.

Tissue salts are listed in the homoeopathic range of medicines, but they are actually quite different, even though the tablets are prepared the same way. Biochemics simply redresses any imbalance in the body's tissue salts whereas homoeopathy uses remedies that induce the symptoms of whatever ailments someone has, to help their body to heal itself: the principle of 'like cures like'.

Kal. phos tissue salts are available from most health shops and some chemists and are small, moulded, lactose-based tablets which dissolve in the mouth. They are absorbed quickly into the bloodstream and give prompt relief to short-term symptoms but need more time to work on long-term problems. Tablets should be taken every half hour for the temporary problems but every two hours over a longer period of time for more persistent problems.

NB: Anyone with a lactose (milk sugar) intolerance shouldn't take the tablets in this form.

Although safe to buy for home use, anyone being treated by a doctor should consult with them before taking tissue salts.

41

DRINK A CUP OF CAMOMILE TEA TO AID RESTFUL SLEEP

TIME: *5 minutes*

INGREDIENTS: *camomile tea bags, hot water, cup, kettle*

METHOD

Simply infuse a camomile tea bag with boiling water as you would any normal tea bag, let it cool and drink. The tea is taken without milk but a small amount of honey can be added if you prefer.

Camomile is a herbal tea made from camomile flowers. It is a plant that has long been recognized in folk medicine, herbal medicine and aromatherapy for its soothing and calming properties. The tea bags also have a dual purpose when it comes to relaxation: you can use them to soothe tired or irritated eyes.

After soaking the tea bags in boiling water, either for tea or not, allow them to cool to skin or a lukewarm temperature, then squeeze out excess water and place one tea bag over each closed eye.

Lie with the bags resting on the eyelids for 10 minutes or so. When you remove them you will find that the eyes are brighter and refreshed: a perfect remedy after a long session in a smoky room or after a late night, when eyes can be tired and irritated.

NB: This could be done in combination with lying in the Alexander position (shortcut 27), where you also have to lie still for 10 to 15 minutes. This way, you will get up with not only an easier neck and spine, but also with rested eyes.

42

TAKE A CUP OF VALERIAN TEA TO ENSURE A DEEP REJUVENATING SLEEP

TIME: *5 minutes*

INGREDIENTS: *valerian root (or valerian in dried form), cup, teaspoon, hot water, kettle, honey, lemon*

METHOD

Grate half a teaspoon of valerian root, or put a quarter teaspoon of its dried form, into a cup and infuse in boiling water.

As the herb tastes slightly bitter on its own, you may find a couple of slices of lemon and a half teaspoon of honey make it more palatable. Alternatively, it can be drunk with a small amount of nutmeg or mixed with peppermint and lemon balm, in which case each would be used in equal proportions – about a quarter teaspoon of each. Sweeten with honey if desired.

Valerian is a potent and fast-acting herbal remedy for stress. Often called nature's tranquillizer, it has a powerful sedative action on the central nervous system. It can also be found in tablet form and is available from most health shops and some pharmacies. You will also find that valerian is one of the ingredients in most herbal tablets that are sold to help sleep, or to calm.

ALTERNATIVE HERBS TO AID SLEEP:

Catnip, lemon balm and vervain are other herbs that can be drunk as tea and are also often used for their mild, sedative properties. They can be used in conjunction with, or instead of, valerian.

43

REDUCE YOUR INTAKE OF CAFFEINE

TIME: *the time it takes to make the decision*

Don't panic. We're talking reduction not abstinence. Coffee and tea both contain caffeine, as do cocoa and most cola drinks. Caffeine is a stimulant, it stimulates the heart, the circulation and causes the kidneys to produce more urine. The immediate effect of having a drink containing caffeine is an instant lift and a reduction of tiredness, which is why so many of us call it our daily shot to get going.

A cup of coffee contains approximately 100–150mg of caffeine, tea 100–125mg, cocoa around 50mg and a cola drink about 40–55mg, depending on the size of the cup it is drunk from.

If the daily intake exceeds 1,000mg, which is about 10 cups of coffee, the following side effects can be experienced: needing to pass water more frequently, restlessness, palpitations, rapid breathing, acid stomach, difficulty sleeping, irritability, and in some cases sweating and headaches.

Caffeine is also addictive and people experience withdrawal symptoms and craving after giving it up. The occasional cup is harmless so without going into complete denial why not start to substitute other drinks during the day, for instance, herbal teas (health shops do a wide variety these days), coffee substitutes (Caro, dandelion coffee), fresh fruit juices or simply good old plain water.

44

FOOD COMBINING FOR A MORE EFFICIENT AND RELAXED DIGESTIVE SYSTEM

TIME: *the time it takes to choose; it is a question of rethinking meals when food shopping then applying the food-combining principles when preparing meals*

INGREDIENTS: *paper and pen, drawing pin to hang the food-combining rules somewhere within sight when preparing food*

Stress affects different people in different ways. If you're someone who suffers from irritable bowel syndrome, discomfort after meals, constipation, bloating, water retention or wind this system of eating will bring relief. It is a programme based on Dr William Hay's theory that the body is more relaxed and comfortable when certain foods are eaten at different times of the day.

METHOD

There are five basic rules to food combining:

1   Don't mix sugar or starch foods with protein or acid fruits at the same meal.

2   Proteins, starches and fats should be eaten in small quantities.

3   Avoid foods which are refined or processed. Use whole grain and unprocessed starches.

4   At least four to four and a half hours should elapse between eating foods from the different groups. The enzymes that digest proteins need an acid environment to act effectively, whereas the enzymes for breaking down starches need an alkaline environment. If these foods are eaten together, the result can be incomplete digestion leading to bloating, discomfort and inadequate absorption of nutrients and elimination of waste products.

5   Increase your intake of fresh fruit and vegetables. There are no forbidden foods but the recommended foods are generally fresh and natural.

NB: Many people are not sure which fruits are 'acid' fruits. This term doesn't refer to their taste but the end product in the body. According to Dr Hay, it is all right to eat some fruits with protein foods. These fruits are: apples, apricots, blueberries, gooseberries, cherries, grapefruit, grapes, lemons, mangoes, oranges, peaches, pears, prunes, raspberries and strawberries. It is also all right to eat some fruits with starches. These are: ripe bananas, figs, ripe papayas, dates, currants, sultanas and raisins.

As many people find it hard to remember which is allowed when, they simply eat fruit in isolation or leave four hours after eating a meal before eating any.

People who follow this diet report that the symptoms of discomfort and bloating disappear and are replaced by a general feeling of good health and well-being. Some people also report an effortless weight loss and relief from arthritis.

45

TEST YOURSELF FOR FOOD ALLERGIES

TIME: *10–15 minutes*

INGREDIENTS: *chair, a willing friend or relative, table, foods that you suspect you may be allergic to, paper and pen to note reactions*

Stress and food allergy can be a vicious circle: allergies can occur more often when under a lot of stress, and a food allergy can lead to depression, fatigue, bloating, lethargy, insomnia, hyperactivity or headaches resulting in stress. To avoid this cycle, test yourself at home to discover what might be the cause.

Although almost any food can cause an allergy, the most common culprits are: dairy products (milk, cheese), eggs, nuts, shellfish, wheat, sugar, chocolate, artificial colourants, foods with additives, and citrus fruits. This simple test often used by kinesiology practitioners can help you identify the food that may be affecting you adversely. You will need the help of a friend or relative to help you carry out the test.

METHOD

1 Sit comfortably and stretch your left arm out in front of you, with your elbow facing out and your fingers and thumb hanging down loosely.

2 Your friend should sit to your right and rest two fingers from their right hand on the wrist of your outstretched arm. At the same time, they should rest their left hand on your right shoulder.

3 Your friend should push down on your wrist while you resist with your arm by pressing upwards. They should continue to press while you both count to five. If you match each other's pressure, and the muscle in your arm felt firm, steady and strong, go on to the next step. (This isn't a wrestling contest or a competition to see who's strongest, so don't overdo it.)

If by any chance your arm moved downwards and felt weak, this muscle is unsuitable for the allergy test and you may need to consult a kinesiology therapist to find another way that you can do the test.

4 Assuming all was well with number three, you are now ready to test with different food substances. Choose a variety of foods, starting with the one that you suspect may be the culprit causing your allergy. Place a sample of the food either under your tongue or just between your lips.

5 Your friend should now place the first two fingers of their left hand on the crease just beneath your right ear whilst at the same time applying pressure on your wrist with their right hand. Again both of you should resist each other's pressure, your friend pressing down, you pressing up. If your arm suddenly feels weak and goes downwards, the chances are you are allergic to the food in your mouth. If you match the pressure as before when you didn't have any food in your mouth, the food substance is OK for you.

Go through your list of foods until you identify the one (if any) that makes the muscle go weak.

6 Once you have identified the food, to double-check that it is having an adverse effect on you, you can do one of two things:

a) next time you eat the food, note your reactions. For example, if the food that made your arm go weak was wheat, note how you feel after eating wheat. Do you get a headache or feel lethargic? If so, it looks like you have found the culprit and should try and avoid it in your diet.

b) Eliminate the suspected food from your diet for one to two weeks. When you reintroduce it, is there any reaction? If so, try to avoid the food in your diet.

NB: If more than one food substance made your arm go downwards, only eliminate one food at a time from your diet or else, when you reintroduce the foods, you won't be able to pinpoint exactly how each food makes you react.

There are other ways of testing food allergies through blood tests but as often allergies and the intensity of their debilitating effect depend on many factors, such as stress levels, vitamin and mineral supplementation and how good your diet is, the allergic reaction may change. A test may tell you that you are allergic to cheese, for example, but a year later, if you are stronger, less stressed and eating a better diet, it may not have such an adverse affect.

This DIY home allergy test can be done easily and you can update your particular allergies and reactions to foods as your circumstances and general health change.

Alternative Shortcuts

46

TAKE FOUR DROPS OF RESCUE REMEDY IN A GLASS OF WATER, SIP FREQUENTLY

TIME: *10 seconds*

INGREDIENTS: *Rescue Remedy, glass, spring water*

Rescue Remedy is excellent for relieving apprehension at times of heightened anxiety, for example, bad news, shock, pre-exam or interview nerves, the grief of a death. It is a natural healer and helps to restore calm, balance and confidence.

It comes in a small bottle, handy for keeping in a handbag or briefcase, and is a combination of five of the flower remedies: impatiens (for frustration/irritability), star of Bethlehem (for shock or fright), cherry plum (for fear of breaking down/losing control), rock rose (for terror) and clematis (for listlessness/feeling vacant).

METHOD

1 Simply add a few drops of the remedy to a glass of spring water and sip at intervals during the day. (The remedy contains brandy to preserve it – some people like to take it straight, just a few drops on the tongue without the spring water!)

These flower remedies were discovered by Dr Edward Bach at the beginning of this century. As an aid to relaxation they are invaluable because they treat and adjust inner feelings that are out of balance. On the shelves of chemists worldwide, there are endless pills and potions to treat physical conditions from headaches to chilblains, but little to treat our inner feelings, aches or emotions as do the Bach flower remedies.

Rescue Remedy is the most widely sold of all the remedies and is available in most health shops around the world. It is a good idea to always carry a bottle of it with you for times of unexpected need.

Dr Bach believed that a healthy emotional state of mind is as important as physical well-being for ensuring lasting good health. He thought that before physical symptoms of disease comes the emotional root of 'dis-ease'. Treat this and you are going to the heart of the problem, instead of waiting until it has manifested itself as a physical complaint.

There are 38 remedies in all which are made from trees, flowers and herbs: these are listed below. All of them can be used to redress any emotional disturbance and help bring about the sense of balance.

THE BACH FLOWER REMEDIES AND, IN BRIEF, THE CONDITIONS THAT THEY CAN AID

Agrimony	mental torture behind carefree mask
Aspen	fears of the unknown, apprehension
Beech	critical, intolerant, complainer
Centaury	weak-willed/subservient
Cerato	needs confirmation from others
Cherry Plum	fear of breaking down or losing control
Chestnut Bud	failure to learn from mistakes
Chicory	selfish/possessive, interfering
Clematis	vacant/listless, distracted
Crab Apple	self-hatred/feeling unclean/ashamed
Elm	overwhelmed by responsibility
Gentian	despondent/negative
Gorse	despair, hopelessness/melancholy
Heather	self-centred
Holly	hatred, jealous, envious, suspicious
Honeysuckle	lives in past, has regrets
Hornbeam	weariness/mental fatigue
Impatiens	impatience, irritability, frustration
Larch	lacks confidence, feels inferior
Mimulus	fear of known things
Mustard	deep gloom/depression for no reason
Oak	despondent but struggling

Olive	total exhaustion
Pine	guilt, blames oneself
Red Chestnut	anxiety for others
Rock Rose	terror
Rock Water	denial, repression
Sceranthus	indecision, mood swings
Star of Bethlehem	shock
Sweet Chestnut	extreme anguish, no hope
Vervain	hyperanxiety, over-effort
Vine	domineering/inflexible
Walnut	oversensitive to change
Water Violet	proud/aloof, mentally rigid
White Chestnut	unwanted thoughts, mental arguments
Wild Oat	uncertainty
Wild Rose	apathy, resignation, no fight left
Willow	resentment

47

STUFF YOUR PILLOW WITH HOPS AND LAVENDER

TIME: *20 minutes to sew muslin bag/5 minutes if you use a pop sock*

INGREDIENTS: *hops, lavender, muslin or cotton, needle and thread, or a 10-denier pop sock*

Hops are a sedative well known for their soothing and tension-relieving properties, and a pillow stuffed with them will help induce a night of deep and relaxed sleep. In days gone by, people often used to sleep on pillows filled with them. As hops have a slightly bitter scent which not everyone likes, to make the scent sweeter people used to mix them with woodruff, lady's bedstraw and meadowsweet, making what was known as a dream pillow.

These days, those ingredients aren't always easy to find, so an effective alternative is to use the hops mixed with lavender. Lavender is also known for its soothing properties and was used in the olden days by French housewives to line their pillows. As its smell is clean and sweet, it would dilute the scent of the hops while their combined properties would make an excellent duo to induce a good night's sleep.

METHOD

1 Sew a square of muslin or fine cotton into a bag (about four inches by four inches is sufficient).

2 Fill the bag with a mixture of the hops and lavender. (You can decide how much of each to put in depending on your liking for either scent.)

3 Sew up the opening and place either in your pillow lining or underneath your pillow.

(Alternatively, buy a pair of 10-denier pop socks and fill the foot of one of them with hops and lavender, then knot the top.)

Hops are also an excellent remedy for a nervous stomach and can be drunk as a tea to calm an agitated digestive system. If the taste is too bitter, add slices of lemon and honey to sweeten.

Hops and lavender are available from most health stores.

48

PASSIONFLOWER CAPSULES

TIME: *just as long as it takes to swallow*

INGREDIENTS: *passionflower capsules, water, glass*

Passiflora or passiflora incarnata is sedative, hypnotic and antispasmodic. It will help unwind and promote deep sleep without any 'hangover' or feeling of drowsiness the next day. Easy to acquire, it is very effective as a natural alternative to chemical tranquillizers and sleeping tablets. It is sold in capsule or tablet form, making it very accessible for people who just want something they can 'take' to help them relax.

You'll find it in most health shops in the section that displays remedies for relaxation or insomnia. Although often called something else like sleepwell or naturacalm, many of the tablets sold to help relaxation are made from extract of passiflora, or passiflora mixed with another natural relaxant.

The dried leaves of the herb can also be bought and drunk as a tea. Because of its antispasmodic properties, it is helpful to anyone suffering from asthma, especially if linked to stress. To make the tea, pour a cup of boiling water onto one teaspoonful and let it infuse for 10 to 15 minutes. To help sleep, drink just before going to bed.

Alternative herbal relaxants for the nervous system are black cohosh, black haw, California poppy, cramp bark, camomile, hops, hyssop, Jamaican dogwood, lady's slipper, lavender, lime blossom, mistletoe, motherwort, pasque flower, rosemary, St John's wort, skullcap and valerian. Most of them are on sale anywhere that sells herbs and natural remedies.

NB: As some people don't like the taste of the herbs, a spoonful of honey and a couple of slices of lemon make most of them more palatable.

49

USE A WHEAT BAG OR LAVENDER BAG TO RELAX ACHING MUSCLES

TIME: *for as long as is comfortable*

INGREDIENTS: *wheatbag, microwave or freezer*

This has to be one of the best inventions to come on the market in a long time. A wheat bag is an easy way of applying moist heat or cold to areas suffering from aches or pains. It is a small soft bag containing therapeutic ingredients such as wheat or lavender (which is known for its soothing properties).

METHOD

The bag can be heated in a microwave in five minutes then applied warm (it stays reassuringly warm for up to 45 minutes), or used as a cold compress by placing in the freezer for a few hours depending on the need. (Inflammation responds best to a cold compress, muscular pain and cramps best to warmth.)

The bag can also be heated in a conventional oven. You either wrap it in tinfoil or put it in a casserole then place it in the prewarmed oven for 10 to 15 minutes, depending on how hot you like it.

The bag comes in two shapes: square, for use on the back or stomach, or sectioned for use on knees, shoulders, the neck, elbows and wrists. It claims to help ease arthritis, back pain, stress and tension around the joints and muscles after exercise and to help relax stomach cramps. It can also be used purely for relaxation.

I'd recommend that if you decide to try the wheat bag that you purchase two at the same time. The sensation of warmth and relaxation derived from one of these is so pleasurable that once a person has hold of one they won't share it! You can drape it round your neck or shoulders and it's like wearing the most wonderful heated collar, place it behind your back as a warm cushion to relieve lower back pain or take it to bed on a cold night to keep you cosy. It can also be wrapped around your knee or other joint or placed on your stomach. Apart from all its therapeutic qualities, it's the ultimate hot water bottle that you wrap around yourself.

An address where you can obtain a wheat bag is supplied at the back in the Useful Addresses section.

50

A VAPOUR RUB TO RELAX AND WARM TIRED MUSCLES

TIME: *2 minutes*

INGREDIENTS: *vapour rub*

A vapour rub with essential or tiger balm can relax and soothe after sports, when you have a headache or when muscles feel tight and tense.

The balm comes in a small pot or tin and is made up of a mixture of healing herbs, spices and oils such as eucalyptus, peppermint, clove, camphor and cinnamon. Because of the warm and menthol properties of some of the oils, the scent is spicy and medicinal.

METHOD

All you do is simply rub a small amount of the balm into the area in need. For headaches, rub it into the temple area; for colds and chest complaints, rub into the chest; for sports strain or aching muscles rub into the legs or arms.

It produces a sensation of warmth on the skin and as the balm is absorbed, it encourages the muscles to gently relax and so eases the strain.

NB: Don't ever rub the balm into areas of skin where there are any cuts or grazes as it will sting or irritate.

The balm can be purchased at most health shops. There is also an address at the back of the book in the Useful Addresses section where you can obtain it by mail order.

51

INHALATION WITH ESSENTIAL OIL OF MARJORAM

TIME: *5 minutes*

INGREDIENTS: *bowl, kettle, water (or steam inhaler), marjoram oil, towel*

This is helpful to those who find that stress affects their breathing and chest area in particular, and also those who suffer from asthma or insomnia.

Marjoram oil is an aromatherapy oil which is derived from the leaves and flowering tops of the plant marjoram. It is particularly beneficial for anyone suffering from any breathing difficulty or chest problem as its actions are warming, sedative, analgesic, comforting and penetrating. It is also a good remedy for insomnia.

The oil has a pleasant warm peppery scent and is appealing to those who don't like the more flowery-scented aromatherapy oils.

METHOD

1 Fill a bowl or basin with boiling water.

2 Add four to six drops of essential oil of marjoram. Remember that its sedative properties may make you feel drowsy, so it is best used at a time when you don't have to go out afterwards.

3 Sit yourself down, lean over the bowl as far as is comfortable and inhale the fumes. Some people find it helpful to put a towel over their head during this process to concentrate the fumes. The oil will soothe and sedate as it enters the system through the lungs and the bloodstream.

An alternative to using a bowl of hot water and towel is to buy a steam inhaler which you can get from most chemists. The main advantage of the inhaler is that it keeps the water hot and the steam consistent whereas if using a bowl of water, it cools quickly. Also, with an inhaler, you can breathe in the scented steam without heating your whole face as they have a special part for just putting your nose into.

NB: Using more than the recommended dose of marjoram oil can dull the senses and continual excessive use of this oil can cause stupefaction so don't overdo it. Other oils that can be used to ease breathing or a tight chest are pine, tea tree and rosemary.

Marjoram oil is available at most health stores and some chemists. There is also an address at the back of the book in the Useful Addresses section where you can obtain the oil by mail order.

52

ADD SIX TO EIGHT DROPS OF LAVENDER OIL TO YOUR EVENING BATH

TIME: *as long as you have to bathe (5 minutes to 30)*
INGREDIENTS: *lavender oil*

Although lavender is one of the most versatile of all the essential oils, with many functions from healing cuts and burns to use as an analgesic, it has long been a favourite for relaxation and stress for various reasons. The oil is extracted from the flowering tops of the lavender plant and has a clean light floral scent which most people find very pleasant. It has sedative properties, which have long been known in the Mediterranean where the women often stuffed their pillows with lavender to encourage sleep (see shortcut 47). A few drops of the oil on a pillow will calm and promote rest for anyone finding it difficult to unwind or suffering from insomnia. The oil rebalances mind and body, helping to regulate the nervous system which may have been aggravated during a stressful day. It re-establishes balance and serenity, promoting a feeling of well-being from which the body can heal itself.

METHOD

1 While the hot tap is running, simply add six to eight drops of essential oil to the water to make an aromatic bath. Swish the oil around in the bath so that it doesn't just lie in one spot on the water.

2 Get in, lie back and breathe in the fragrant air and let the healing properties of the oil float the tensions of the day away.

The idea behind aromatherapy is to get the essential oil into the bloodstream. This can be done in different ways such as massage, use of compresses, steam inhalation (see shortcut 51) or by an aromatic bath.

The bath method is the simplest as nothing more is required than to add the drops of essential oil to the water then lie back and enjoy. And the oil is much more than just a pleasant scent in the bathroom. As you breathe in the aroma which is released into the atmosphere through the heat of the water and the steam, the lavender enters the lungs from where it will be absorbed into the bloodstream and into the body's system. Then its healing properties can go to work promoting rest, relaxation and encouraging a deep and replenishing sleep.

Alternative oils that can be used to relax in an aromatic bath include camomile, clary sage, marjoram, melissa, neroli, patchouli, sandalwood, rosewood, rose, vetivert and ylang ylang. Spend some time in a local health shop deciding which scents you like as some will appeal more than others to different individuals. All these oils will have a therapeutic and relaxing effect and can be used either on their own or in combination with one or two of the others.

For men who perhaps don't like the light scent of lavender, sandalwood would be a pleasing alternative. It is used as a base in many men's colognes and aftershaves. It can be used on its own or in combination with lime and lavender (which is also a popular mix for men's colognes).

NB: Don't use more than six to eight drops in a bath because although made from flowers, barks and herbs, oils are potent substances and using too much can irritate or burn the skin.

Lavender oil can be obtained at most health stores and some chemists. There is also an address at the back of the book in the Useful Addresses section where you can obtain the oil by mail order.

53

TAKE A HOMOEOPATHIC REMEDY

TIME: *just as long as it takes to swallow*

INGREDIENTS: *variable according to individual*

Although it is difficult to pinpoint just one remedy because each person's symptoms and lifestyle are looked at individually, homoeopathy cannot be overlooked as an aid to fighting stress because it has so much to contribute.

Homoeopathy was founded by Dr Samuel Hahnemann who was an eighteenth-century physician and chemist. He was disillusioned by the methods in medicine that were prevalent in his time and, being convinced of the body's ability to mend itself, he set about researching a more natural and gentle alternative to healing.

There are three main principles to homoeopathy:

1 The law of similars – that like can heal like, and the belief that taking minute amounts of mineral, herbal or animal toxins stimulates the body's healing power. If these same doses were given to a healthy person, they would produce the same symptoms that the unwell person is complaining of.

2 That no two people's symptoms are exactly alike. For example, three people may be suffering from a headache. For one, it may be the result of emotional tension and inner anxiety, for another it may be the result of mental fatigue and strained back and neck muscles through bad posture and prolonged sitting at a desk, for another it may be the result of eating and drinking excessively. In homoeopathy, all three would be given a different remedy according to their different symptoms, rather than all being given a tablet generally for headaches.

3 That the symptoms are usually a sign of an underlying problem and imbalance and this must be taken into account by looking at an individual's overall life, physical, mental and emotional health.

A visit to a homoeopathic doctor will start with the doctor making a very detailed account of a patient's overall health and lifestyle. The more specific the account, the more it helps. From this, the doctor will choose the remedy that he feels is right for that patient at that time. (Once they have taken their account and know your type, no matter what comes up in the future, they will be able to recommend a remedy specifically for you at that time.)

The remedies are also available in chemists and health shops nationwide and can be sold over the counter without you having to have seen a doctor. Although there are as many as 60 remedies in common use (and as many as 3,000 in use throughout the world), listed below are just some of the remedies that are helpful to stress-related problems. Without specific details, it can only be a very rough guide to which one is best and can really only serve as an introduction to how broad and thorough the range of remedies is. For example, if stressed, a different remedy would be recommended depending on how it has affected you. Can you sleep? Are you irritable? Overcritical? Burned out? Feeling insecure? Overemotional? Is the stress due to bad news or an emotional upset, and so on. Look through and if any of the remedies match your symptoms, that may well be the one for you to try. However, if you have time, a visit to a homoeopathic practitioner would be worthwhile in pinpointing the exact remedy in your particular case.

Homoeopathy is a gentle medicine and won't cause any harmful side effects if the wrong remedy is taken. However, if you choose the right remedy, an improvement is often felt immediately. (Some people also feel an immediate worsening of the symptoms followed by a marked improvement.) The remedy is taken in the form of a small pill which dissolves on the tongue.

SOME HOMOEOPATHIC REMEDIES

Aconite 6	for fear, shock, panic, anxiety, anger
Actea rac. 6	for headaches, depression, painful muscles, shooting pains
Argent nit. 6	for headaches, anticipatory fear, mental strain
Arnica	for mental and physical shock, sore muscles, back pain
Arsen, alb. 6	for restlessness
Ac.phos	for weakness and depression due to stress
Aurum	for depression
Belladonna	for throbbing headache, irritability
Calc. carb. 6	for cramp, depression
Carbo vegetablis	for hangovers, indigestion, exhaustion
Calc. phos. 6	for mental and general debility
Chamomilla	for irritability, restlessness
Coffea 6	for insomnia due to mental activity, tension
Gelsemium 6	for fears and phobias, tight headache, nervous anxiety
Ignatia 6	for stress due to shock, bereavement, hysteria, loss of appetite
Kali. phos 6	for nervous exhaustion, indigestion, exhaustion to the point of giddiness
Lycopodium 6	for anxiety, excessive hunger, headaches
Nux Vom. 6	for apprehension, irritability, nervous indigestion
Pulsatilla 6	for weepiness, depression, headaches
Rhus tox 6	for backache after physical exhaustion
Sciatica	for restlessness, nervousness
Sepia 6	for depression often caused by menopause

NB: Avoid the use of mint, menthol and coffee for at least 24 hours after taking a remedy as they interfere with its potency. Only try one remedy at a time.

54

A VAPORIZER WITH OIL OF VETIVERT FOR RELIEVING ANXIETY AND INDUCING SLEEP

TIME: *2 minutes to prepare*

INGREDIENTS: *vetivert oil, pot vaporizer, night-light, matches, water*

Burning essential oil in a room can be used not only to scent the atmosphere but also to create an air of relaxation or stimulation depending on which oil is used. Essential oil of vetivert is known as the oil of tranquillity. It is good for relieving anxiety, nervous tension and insomnia. As with sandalwood, vetivert is often used in men's colognes and is a popular choice with them because of its woody base scent in contrast to some of the more floral alternatives.

A vaporizer is a small pottery bowl that has two levels. The lower level has enough room for a candle or night-light and the top level has a small shelf where you can put the oil or water that you want to heat.

METHOD

1 Put the vaporizer in the room that you want to scent, put a candle in place on the lower level and light it.

2 Fill the top shelf of the vaporizer with water then add four drops of essential oil of vetivert. As the water and oil warm, the oil will scent the atmosphere. (Although you could put the oil straight onto the shelf, the fragrance lasts longer if it is mixed with a little water.)

3 As you sit or lie in the scented room and breathe in, the oil will enter the system through the lungs and bloodstream.

Alternative oils that can be used for relaxation, depending on people's personal preferences of scent, are (as for shortcut 52) camomile, clary sage, marjoram, melissa, neroli, patchouli, sandalwood, rosewood, rose and ylang ylang.

Vetivert oil is available at most health stores and some chemists. There is also an address at the back of the book in the Useful Addresses section where you can obtain the oil by mail order. Vaporizers can also be bought from most health stores or by mail order from most suppliers of aromatherapy oils.

55

COOL TIRED FEET IN A FOOTBATH WITH ESSENTIAL OIL OF PEPPERMINT

TIME: *10 minutes*

INGREDIENTS: *large (or washing-up) bowl, cold water, peppermint oil, towel*

This is the best remedy in the world for hot, tired swollen feet. Peppermint oil is an aromatherapy oil which has many healing properties, including being antiphlogostic (reduces inflammation) and cooling. The oil is extracted from the whole of the peppermint plant and also acts as a stimulant. It can be used to revitalize not only feet but the whole system (it is often used as an oil when someone has fainted, to help them revive).

METHOD

1 Simply fill a bowl with cold water and add four to six drops of the essential oil of peppermint. Swish the oil around so that it doesn't all gather in one spot.

2 Put your bare feet in the water, sit back, soak them and relax for 10 minutes or so.

This is perfect for times when you've been on your feet all day. As you sit relaxing and inhaling the refreshing minty menthol scent, the oil will also enter the bloodstream via the lungs and the skin of the feet, and act on your whole being, renewing energy and clearing away fatigue.

NB: Peppermint oil should not be used if you are pregnant, or if you are taking a course of homoeopathic medicines: it acts as an antidote to them.

It is available at most health stores and some chemists. There is also an address at the back of the book in the Useful Addresses section where you can obtain the oil by mail order.

56

A DO-IN PRESSURE POINT MASSAGE TO RELIEVE EXHAUSTION AND REVITALIZE

TIME: *5–10 minutes*

INGREDIENTS: *chair*

Do-in is a Chinese form of self-massage which can relieve tension and revitalize the system. It works on pressure points along the channels of energy called meridians which are used by acupuncture and shiatsu practitioners. I first came across it 10 years ago when I was doing a course on anatomy and physiology. After lunch, the teacher was well aware that her students weren't as focused as they had been in the morning session and that concentration was flagging. She'd get us all up and run through the following process. It immediately woke us up and revitalized us, ready for the afternoon's study.

The simple exercise process can be done anywhere at any time of the day for immediate effect and is particularly useful if you're at work and feeling sluggish, and in need of a quick remedy.

METHOD

1   Stretch out your palm. Bend your middle finger to touch the centre of the palm. The point it touches is your pressure point. With the thumb of your other hand, apply pressure for 10 to 15 seconds to the spot in the centre of your palm. Then alternate hands so that you apply pressure to the same spot on the other palm. Repeat three to four times.

　　　　This will relieve exhaustion, high blood pressure and low energy.

2   Find the point in the web of the right hand between the right thumb and index finger. With the left thumb on top and index finger beneath (on the palm side), apply pressure, gently rotating the left thumb for 15 to 20 seconds. This relieves indigestion and can revitalize. Repeat on the left hand, using the right thumb and index finger to find the web, apply pressure then rotate the right thumb on top of the web between the left thumb and index finger.

3 Reach down to your lower leg. Measure four fingers' width up from the ankle bone. This is your pressure point. Apply pressure for 10 to 15 seconds then do the same on the other leg. Repeat three times.

This is good if you're having difficulty sleeping and is also good for digestive problems and PMT.

4 Next, find the points on the face that are on your cheekbones directly under where your pupils are if you are looking ahead. Press in with the index fingers from both hands (you can rotate slightly on the spot if you like for added pressure and relief). This brings relief to facial tension.

5 Clench your hand into a fist and with your wrist loose, lightly tap a line along the top of your shoulder, the side of your neck and down your back as far as you can reach. Now do it with a firm tap. Do this for 20 seconds, tracing along the line, then repeat on the other side. This will alleviate tension in the neck, shoulder and upper back. You can also lightly tap over your head from one ear to the other. This will help you feel more alert and energized.

6 Now, with the same fist position, tap along the inner line from the hand to the armpit. Repeat on the other arm. Then with the same light taps, trace along the outer arm from shoulder to hand. Repeat on the other side. Repeat three to four times on each arm.

7 If your legs feel tense from sitting in one position for a long time, you can do this same tapping, moving from the feet to the top of the leg on the inside of the leg, and from the top of the leg to the feet whilst working on the outer side of the leg. (For the front of the body and inside of arms and legs, move up the body. For the back and outside of arms and legs, move down the body.)

NB: Don't try any of these techniques on inflamed or infected areas.

For further lessons in this self-help technique there is an address at the back of the book in the Useful Addresses section where you can find out where to attend classes.

57

A DIY SHIATSU MASSAGE FOR THE FACE

TIME: *5 minutes*

INGREDIENTS: *table, chair*

This facial massage can completely change the way you feel in a few minutes. It is effective for headaches or mental stress from concentrating hard over a prolonged period of time.

METHOD

1 Rest your elbows on your desk or table. Keep them here in all stages up to number 10. This will steady your hands and help you apply pressure when it comes to doing the acupressure points on the face.

2 Trace the points (see diagram) directly above the eyebrow with the index finger. Rest your thumb on the inner end of your eyebrow and with the index finger, trace along just above the eyebrow, stopping every eighth of an inch to apply pressure with your index finger. This can be done by leaning your head into the finger. Repeat on the other side, again stopping each eighth of an inch along to apply pressure with the index finger.

3 Rest the index finger on top of the eyebrow and put your thumb under the ridge. This time, you'll use your thumb to apply pressure. Trace along the line under the eyebrow on the ridge of the eye socket, stopping every eighth of an inch to apply pressure by leaning into the thumb. Repeat on the other eye, again stopping to apply pressure with the thumb every eighth of an inch.

4 Rest the thumb just below the ear and bring your fingers up to the bridge of your nose. With the index finger, trace the line of the ridge of the socket under the eye stopping to apply pressure each eighth of an inch along with your index finger. Repeat on the other side, again applying pressure with the index finger each eighth of an inch.

5 Rest your fingers mid-forehead and with the thumb, trace five lines from the end of the eyebrow out to the hairline. Apply pressure at points up the line (as shown in the diagram) with the thumb. Repeat on the other side, again applying pressure with the thumb at each point.

6 Still with your hands in this position, rotate clockwise on the temple with the thumb.

7 Put fingers on tops of the eyebrow and with the thumbs, apply pressure in the inner corner of the upper eye ridge. Hold for a few moments (this is a powerful acupressure point and you'll know it when you feel it as it is quite strong).

8 Slide the fingers down to the bridge of your nose and with the index fingers, press along points on the side of the nose and cheekbones as shown in the diagram. Stop every eighth of an inch to lean down into the elbows, so applying pressure.

9 Next, with one index finger, trace the line from mid-eyebrows up to the hairline, as shown in the diagram. Apply pressure with your finger at regular intervals along the line until you reach the top.

10 Finish off by slightly bowing your head and lifting your elbows up. Hold your head with your fingers and with your thumbs reach for the bony ridge at the back of your skull. Start with both thumbs in the middle and trace the line, applying pressure with your thumbs along the ridge from the centre to behind the ears as shown in the diagram.

11 Lift head upright again and take a deep breath. You will find that you feel much lighter and more energized.

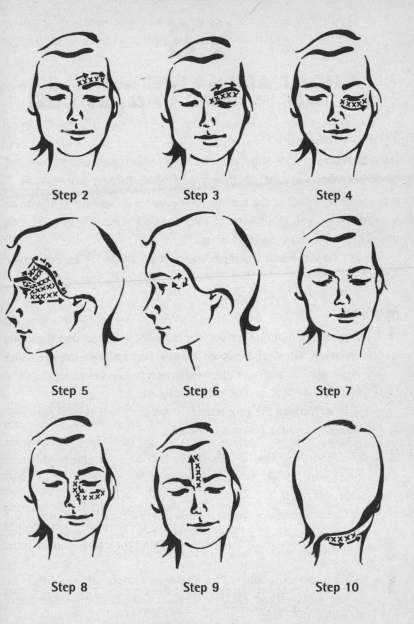

Step 2

Step 3

Step 4

Step 5

Step 6

Step 7

Step 8

Step 9

Step 10

Shiatsu massage for the face

58

A HOME AROMATHERAPY BACK MASSAGE WITH OIL OF CLARY SAGE

TIME: *20–30 minutes*

INGREDIENTS: *clary sage oil, base oil (either grapeseed, almond, apricot kernel, olive or sunflower oil), bowl, tablespoon, towels*

If you can't afford either the time or the money for an appointment with an aromatherapist, you don't have to miss out on the benefit of relaxation that an aromatherapy massage gives.

Simply follow the instructions below with a partner for an easy-to-do massage at home.

METHOD

1   Prepare the room where you are to do the massage. Dim the lights and make sure that the room is warm. Perhaps have some relaxing music playing and have plenty of towels to hand to cover the parts of the body that you're not working on.

Read through the process before you start so that you're familiar with what you're going to be doing.

2   Mix your oil. Use a tablespoon of base oil (one of those mentioned above) with four drops of the essential oil of clary sage added to it.

Clary sage is a wonderful oil as it relaxes almost to the point of euphoria. It has a pleasing nutty aroma and is good for stress and tension and acts as a muscle relaxant.

3   Ask the person about to be massaged to take off their shirt or blouse and lie down on their stomach and get comfortable. Kneel down by their side.

4 Place the palm of one hand on the top of the spine and the other palm on the base of the spine. Hold like this with gentle pressure for a moment or two. It is a good way to start as it tells the body that it is about to be worked on, feels very reassuring and is gentler than just plunging in with a long sweeping movement.

5 Put the oil on your hands to start and lightly apply all over the back. Now place your hands on either side on the base of the spine and sweep up to the top and around to the shoulders. Do it slowly. Repeat this a few times.

6 Work on the lower back, again with your hands on either side of the base of the spine. Trace a line starting at the inside of the waist and work out along the hips. Repeat a few times then, following the same line, place your hands down and lean in for a moment as you move along, putting your weight behind your hands.

7 Repeat step five taking care at all times not to put pressure on the spine.

8 Knead the shoulders, one at a time, as though kneading dough, rolling the flesh and releasing. Do this a few times on either shoulder.

9 Go back to the long sweeping movements that cover the whole back.

10 Finish by lightly placing one index finger on the top of the spine and the other on the base of the spine. Hold like this for a minute. It may feel to you as though nothing is happening but it will feel incredibly relaxing to the person receiving the massage.

11 Let whoever's being massaged lie quietly for a while; they may even want to fall asleep. Advise them not to shower the oil off as essential oil takes six to eight hours to be thoroughly absorbed into the system through the skin and bloodstream, where it can continue its good work long after the massage has finished.

If you want to develop your technique, there are a few basic strokes that you can bring into the process, varying the speed and pressure:

a) **Effleurage** – the long sweeping strokes done with both hands together or one palm on top of the other hand;

b) **Percussion** – short, fast, rhythmic movement done with the sides of the hand in a chopping motion. This is good for fleshy areas like the buttocks, shoulders or thighs (never the spine);

c) **Petrissage** – grasping and squeezing and kneading certain parts of the muscle. Flesh is picked up like bread dough and gently rolled and released, which is good for muscle relief;

d) **Friction** – small, circular movements made by one or more fingers, the pads of the thumb and the heels of the hand.

Alternatively, you can buy one of the many massage videos now available and massage along with the presenter until you've got the hang of it. It is often easier to pick up the strokes if you can actually see them being demonstrated.

TIPS

- Go slowly. Don't rush, as there's nothing worse than having a massage and feeling that the masseur wants to get it over with.
- Vary the strokes, using different speeds and pressures. For example, you can do the sweeping strokes fast or slow or even slower. You can do them lightly or lean harder.
- Use your body weight behind your hands. If you try to work more deeply by only using your hands, you'll get tired. It feels much better when you lean into the strokes.
- Decide the pressure between you before starting, as some people like it done very lightly, others like it done hard.
- In winter, warm the oil on a radiator, as it adds to the luxurious feel. Also, heat towels on the radiator as it feels wonderful to be swathed in warm towels whilst fragrant oils waft up to your nose.
- Be confident.

NB: Alternative oils for stress are lavender, marjoram, rosewood, sandalwood, neroli, camomile, ylang ylang, melissa, patchouli, rose and geranium.

Choose the most appealing oil for your massage.

You could also integrate the techniques and movements from shortcuts 56, 57, 59, 61, 62 and 63 into this massage to make it a longer session.

Clary sage oil is available at most health stores and some chemists. There is also an address at the back of the book in the Useful Addresses section where you can obtain the oil by mail order.

59

A RELAXING HEAD MASSAGE
WITH ESSENTIAL OIL OF MELISSA

TIME: *10 minutes*

INGREDIENTS: *melissa oil, base oil (apricot kernel, almond, olive, sunflower or grapeseed oil), blanket or towel*

A soothing head massage with melissa oil can relax and revitalize even the most angst-ridden person.

Melissa oil is a perfect oil to use to ease away deep anxiety as it is renowned for its calming properties and its ability to help lower blood pressure and chase away black thoughts. In days gone by, women used to plait melissa in the hair of young brides on their wedding day to help stave off pre-marriage nerves.

METHOD

1 Mix half a tablespoon of base oil in a bowl. This is used to dilute the essential oil.

2 Add two to three drops of melissa oil and stir it in. It is a potent oil and this small amount is absolutely sufficient. Any more could irritate the skin.

3 Put a blanket or towel on the floor and ask the person about to be massaged to lie down on their back. You can support the head with a folded towel.

4 Sit at the top of the person's head and apply a little of the oil to your hands, just enough to cover the scalp lightly.

Before you begin the massage, place your hands on either side of the person's head, palms on each temple. Hold their head like this for a moment as this can be very soothing and is a gentler start to the process than jumping straight in with the massage strokes.

5 To begin with, make slow circular movements on the scalp just above the hairline on either side of the head with both hands. Rotate and knead with your fingers as you would if washing your hair.

Do this slowly, deeply and gently. (Think about all the times you've had your hair washed at the hairdresser and what a difference it makes when you get a washer who takes their time and doesn't scrub your head as if they want to get it over with.) Think now about how you'd like it to feel. Cover the head with these movements. (The best way to know what feels soothing is to swop with a friend, and sometimes be the giver of the massage, sometimes the receiver. You soon get a good idea of what feels best and just how slow you can go for it to be effective.)

6 When you have covered the head in the gentle circular kneading, cup the right ear with your right hand and gently turn the head to the left. Now continue your movements with your left hand getting right in at the base of the scalp and skull. When you have finished the right side (spend a good few minutes doing it), turn the head to the right and do the same on the left side of the scalp with your right hand. Remember the slower you do it, the calmer the person feels.

7 Imagine someone has drawn lines on the scalp from the base of the skull to the forehead where the hair stops. Imagine that these lines are about half an inch apart as you are going to work up them with your thumb. Again hold the head firmly with both hands cupping underneath and gently turn the head slowly to the right. (If there is any resistance in the neck or the person complains of pain, don't force it. Stop and do what you can with the head in a central position.)

Trace the first imaginary line on the left-hand side with your left thumb. This will be from behind the left ear up to just over the left ear. Work from the base of the skull upwards. Stop at inchly intervals along this line and apply a little pressure with your thumb. Hold for a moment then move up the line.

Keep a light hold on the head with the unused fingers of your left hand: the more secure the head feels, the more the person receiving the massage can feel safe and at ease. If they feel you might drop their head at any moment, they won't let go and relax.

8 Trace these imaginary lines at half an inch apart all the way up to the centre of the scalp, each time starting at the base of the skull and slowly moving up to the top.

9 When you have reached the centre, turn the head to the left and repeat the same process again, this time with the right hand.

10 When you have done this, gently turn the head back to the centre and lower it slowly back on to the towel. Then cup each of your palms on either side of the head again (on the temples). Hold for a minute. These 'holds' may seem as though nothing is happening to the giver of the massage but are extremely soothing for the recipient, giving them a chance to feel relaxed and inhale the scent of the oil on your hands.

11 If you need to put a little more oil on your hands do so and repeat the slow, general, all-over head rub again with circular kneading movements.

12 When this is finished, lower the head back onto the towel and slide your hands, palms up, underneath to the base of the skull. Line your fingers along the ridge at the base of the skull and with the slightest lift pull up and towards you (only about half an inch, if that) very gently and hold for a minute. Having one's head cupped and held like this, whilst inhaling the tranquillizing oil, is one of the most relaxing experiences a person can have.

After a minute, lower the head and finish by putting your palms, one over the other, on the recipient's forehead for 10 seconds.

13 Tell the person to get up when they feel like it, that there is no hurry. The chances are they will stay there for a while and have a bit of a sleep, in which case ensure that they are warm enough and provide a blanket to cover them.

NB: As the hair of the person who's had the massage will be a little oily afterwards, it is best to try and time this treatment for when they don't have to get up, wash their hair and dash off anywhere. As all aromatherapy oils take between six to eight hours to be absorbed into the system, the best time to have this short massage would be at night-time: the melissa oil could be left on overnight and the recipient will get maximum benefit from it.

If the person having the massage has long hair, ask them to leave it loose, as that way you can easily access the scalp. If they keep it tied up, it is difficult to do the movements without pulling on the hair.

Alternative oils that could be used which also have tranquillizing properties are marjoram, camomile and lavender. They should also be diluted in a base oil before application to the skin or scalp.

Melissa oil is available at most health stores and some chemists. There is also an address at the back of the book in the Useful Addresses section where you can obtain the oil by mail order.

60

USE A COLD COMPRESS WITH ESSENTIAL OIL OF ROSEMARY TO RELIEVE A STRESS HEADACHE

TIME: *5 minutes*

INGREDIENTS: *rosemary oil, cold water, bowl, small towel or flannel*

Rosemary oil is used because of its ability to ease stress; it is also a natural analgesic (pain reliever). It has a light, medicinal, herbal scent which is pleasing to both male and female sense of smell.

METHOD

1 Put some cold water in a bowl and add four to six drops of the essential oil of rosemary. Swish the oil around so that it doesn't just gather in one spot.

2 Put a small towel or flannel in the scented water, let it soak until completely wet and cool, then remove it and wring out most of the moisture. Fold it into a strip thin enough to cover the forehead and long enough to fall by the sides of the head.

3 Lie the person with the tension headache on a flat surface (on a blanket on the floor will do), then apply the cold compress to the forehead. When it is in position, take either end of the compress in your hands, pull it tight, then pull down to the sides of the head and lean on it with your weight so that it causes pressure on the forehead. Stay like this for six to eight seconds. The combination of the cool compress, the healing oil and slightly menthol scent, plus the pressure to the forehead, is immensely soothing.

4   After the six to eight seconds, lift the whole compress off the head. You will be surprised how much heat is transmitted from the head to the towel and it reduces tension for the headache sufferer.

5   Soak the compress once more and repeat the whole process.

6   After a couple of times on the forehead, soak the towel in the scented water and wring out again. This time lift the head very gently and put the towel round the back of the neck.

7   Taking an end in either hand, lift about half an inch and tug very gently. This also brings great relief and ease to an aching head: the neck and forehead are the main focal areas for tense headaches and are therefore the areas that most need relief.

Alternative oils that can be used for this process are lavender and peppermint, both renowned for their ability to lift stress and ease headaches. If you have all three oils in the bathroom cabinet, it may help to let the headache sufferer sniff each bottle to see which scent appeals the most at that particular time (people often know instinctively which oil is going to help them the most and are attracted to it).

NB: Peppermint shouldn't be used if on a course of homoeopathy as it acts as an antidote. It should also be avoided if pregnant.

Rosemary oil is available at most health stores and some chemists. There is also an address at the back of the book in the Useful Addresses section where you can obtain the oil by mail order.

61

APPLY PRESSURE TO THE SOLAR PLEXUS REFLEXOLOGY POINT WHILST TAKING DEEP SLOW BREATHS

TIME: *5 minutes*

This simple reflexology technique is very effective in calming someone down in an instant. It helps breathe out the stress whilst releasing the tight feeling from the solar plexus area.

METHOD

1   Lie the stressed person down. Hold one of their feet and find the point marked on the diagram, in the centre just beneath the ball of the foot. You will feel a natural indentation there when you put your finger on it.

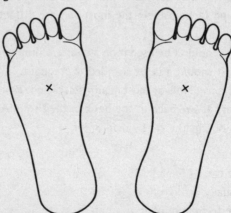

This is the point for the solar plexus in reflexology and is a common place for stress and tension to gather.

2   Either kneel or sit at the person's feet so that you are comfortable and find the points on both feet.

3   With your thumbs firmly on the point and your fingers resting on the top of the foot so that you have a secure hold, ask the person to breathe in slowly and deeply into their abdomen.

As they inhale, begin to apply pressure to the solar plexus point, then hold, and count slowly up to four.

4   Now, still holding the point, ask the person to exhale slowly. As they breathe out, slowly take your thumbs away from the points. As you do, count again up to four. Pause.

5   Repeat this process several times and you will find the person has calmed down considerably.

Often when under stress, people only breathe from the upper lung; as a result, tension that ought to be breathed out gathers under the ribcage in the solar plexus, causing discomfort, a tense stomach and the overall sensation of a waist band of tightness. The solar plexus is an extremely sensitive part of the body. In fact, an animal will only show its solar plexus to you when it feels it can completely trust you. It is a storehouse for many conscious and unconscious feelings and emotions.

Reflexology is a method used to activate the natural healing powers of the body and a full treatment has many benefits including improved circulation, relaxation and a general feeling of well-being. It was used by the ancient Chinese, Indians, Japanese and Egyptians, the basic theory being that there are certain points on the feet that correspond to other parts of the body, and that by applying pressure to one of these points on the foot, you are also treating the part it corresponds to as well as stimulating the body's healing potential.

Although, usually, a full reflexology treatment will take between 40 and 60 minutes, the technique of the thumb press can be very simply carried out in minutes and is most effective.

62

FAST RELIEF FOR THE BACK WITH PRESSURE-POINT MASSAGE

TIME: *5–10 minutes*

INGREDIENTS: *blanket or towel*

This easy massage along pressure points on the back will help relieve strain and tension held in the back area.

METHOD

1 Put a blanket or towel on the floor and ask the recipient to lie face-down with their arms by their sides. They can keep their clothes on for this if they wish as it can be done through clothing.

Make sure that there is enough room for you to move comfortably around the body on your knees.

2 Kneel at the recipient's head and, without applying any pressure, lightly trace the spine to feel exactly where it is.

3 Then, starting at the top of the spine, place your palms on either side of it. Ask the person to breathe in slowly; then kneel back into your calves and kneel up, lean over, and ask the person to begin to exhale. Start to apply pressure with the palms of your hands to the back area.

As you begin to apply the pressure, the other person should be breathing out. Now you can start to lean in a little more, slowly putting your weight behind your palms as you do so. Keep the pressure equal on both sides of the spine and don't just push with your palms. It feels much better for the recipient if you lean in with your body weight, gradually increasing the pressure as you do so. Don't hurry it, and when you are leaning in, hold that position for a few moments.

4   Ask the person to inhale again, lift your hands and move down a palm's length.

    Repeat exactly the same process moving down a palm's length at a time until you reach the base of the spine.

5   Midway, you may find it easier to move yourself alongside the body to finish off the lower back.

    Each time, synchronize the application of pressure with the person's slow breathing out.

6   When you have finished doing the process with your palms, go back to the top and begin again, this time using your thumbs. As with the palms, don't push with the thumbs; rather, lean in letting the pressure build up as you kneel up and put the weight of your body behind the thumbs. (You will also find it less tiring to do this way.)

7   When you have finished leaning in to the points alongside the spine with your thumbs, ask the other person to take a few breaths before getting up. When they do get up, they should roll onto their side, bend their knees and get into a sitting position, then stand up slowly.

NB: At no time should you apply pressure to the actual spine; only press along either side of the spine as shown in the diagram.

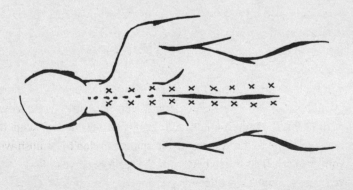

Pressure points along the side of the spine. Do not apply pressure to the actual spine itself.

Massage with finger pressure is known as shiatsu and is a healing art from Japan. In a full shiatsu treatment, pressure is applied to acupuncture points located on the meridian lines all over the body. These lines carry what is call chi around the body. Chi means the life force. In the same way that our blood vessels carry blood around the body, the meridian lines carry energy. Each line corresponds to a bodily function and if they get blocked through strain or stress then that bodily function doesn't work as well as it could. The shiatsu pressure helps release blocks, reduces stress held in the body, and rebalances the body's energy.

For details of where you can find a shiatsu practitioner for a full body treatment turn to the back of the book to the Useful Addresses section.

63

A COMPRESS OF CAMOMILE ESSENTIAL OIL AND MASSAGE FOR THE SOLAR PLEXUS AND ABDOMEN

TIME: *5–10 minutes*

INGREDIENTS: *camomile oil, small bowl, base oil (apricot kernel, almond, olive, sunflower or grapeseed oil), hot water, teaspoon, small towel, pillow to support knees*

The solar plexus is a common area for many people to hold their stress. This can result in the feeling of a nervous stomach, shallow breathing and general anxiety.

The following process can help relieve stress and induce relaxation and can be done as a self-massage or carried out by a friend.

METHOD

1 Prepare your oil: – Put a teaspoon of base oil (see above) in a small cup. Add three drops of camomile oil. Warm the oil as this adds to the relaxing effect: the sensation of warm oil is more pleasurable than cold. In winter this is easily done by simply placing your container on a radiator for a minute or two.

Essential oil of camomile is renowned for its emotionally calming effect and its ability to soothe internal inflammatory conditions such as colitis, gastritis and diarrhoea (stress can often be the root cause behind these complaints).

2 Lie down on your back but keep the knees bent or supported with a pillow. Apply a little of the oil to your hands (if doing a self-massage) and gently cover the area of the abdomen.

Starting on the right-hand side of the body, trace a line by stroking with the tips of your fingers up the side of the body, from just above the hip-bone to just under the ribcage on the right; then stroke across under the ribcage, across the solar plexus to the left side then down the left of the body, stopping just above the hip-bone. Repeat this motion several times, very slowly and very gently. After a few times, you can repeat using a little finger pressure every inch or so along this line.

You are tracing the direction of the large colon, so always go from right and up, across to the left and down.

3 Find the solar plexus, which is located in the middle of the upper abdomen in the space at the base of the ribcage. Breathe in, then, as you breathe out, press down with the tips of your fingers on this area and sweep gently away with the whole hand using the palms. Repeat several times, each time synchronizing the sweep away with the exhalation.

4 Repeat the first movement from the right of the abdomen to the left but this time use your whole hand. Sweep with one hand after the other and as you go around let the circles you are tracing become more central, taking you slowly into the centre of the abdomen and around the navel so that in the end the whole area has been swept.

5 Finish off with a warm compress. Put a pint of hot water in a bowl or basin. Add four drops of camomile oil and soak a small towel or flannel in the water. When soaked, wring the compress out. Lie back again and apply it to the solar plexus and abdomen area. Lie like this for five minutes until the compress has cooled.

The combination of the warmth to this area and the soothing oil can be very effective in calming a stressed person, particularly someone who holds their stress here. Also, the heat of the towel on the area that has just been oiled will help the absorption of the camomile oil already on the skin into the bloodstream; when you get up, the process will continue to benefit you as the oil enters the system via the bloodstream.

Alternative oils that could be used are marjoram and lavender, which are also known for their soothing properties.

Camomile oil is available at most health stores and some chemists. There is also an address at the back of the book in the Useful Addresses section where you can obtain the oil by mail order.

64

TREAT YOURSELF TO A REFLEXOLOGY TREATMENT FOR RELAXATION

TIME: *40–50 minutes*

INGREDIENTS: *diary, pen, phone*

Reflexology is a wonderful treatment for stress and anxiety as it is deeply relaxing and helps to restore the body's energy, well-being and natural vitality. It is also an excellent relaxation alternative for anyone who doesn't like to have body massage, yet recognizes the need for some kind of treatment to help them to unwind. Forty minutes of reflexology can be as beneficial for stress as an hour's body massage.

Some people don't like to remove their clothing for massage, others don't like their bodies to be touched. For reflexology, you remain clothed except for the feet which are usually lightly sprinkled with talcum powder before a session begins.

The origins of reflexology can be traced back as far as 5,000 years ago in China; there are also records of the Japanese, Indians and Egyptians working on the feet to promote good health. It is based on the theory that certain points or zones on the feet correspond to different parts and organs of the body so by treating the foot, you are in fact affecting the whole body.

There are 10 energy zones running all over the body to the feet and any disorders can be put down to a blockage in one of these channels. As the reflex points on the foot that correspond to these zones are worked on, these blocks can be removed and energy can flow naturally again, restoring balance to mind and body.

A reflexologist will gently apply pressure and massage each foot in turn, with the thumbs and fingers, while at the same time determining where the problem areas and weaknesses are in the body. There are more than 7,000 nerve endings in the foot that interconnect with every part of the body.

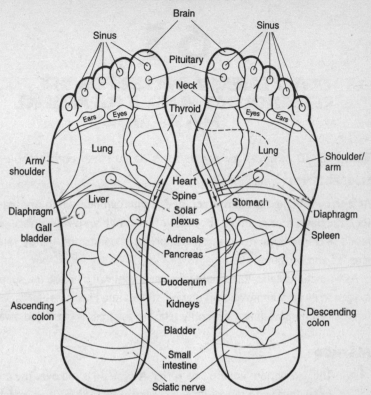

Points on the soles of the feet according to reflexology

These are stimulated during treatment and this encourages the opening and clearing of the neural pathways leading to the brain and spinal cord and in turn to the organs and muscles. The overall treatment tunes the body, improves circulation and induces a feeling of well-being.

For the person being treated, a weakness in an area of the body will show up as discomfort on the corresponding point on the foot. The reflexologist will feel it as tiny granules or crystals in the area and apply gentle pressure. This disperses the discomfort, bringing relief and a feeling of relaxation to the body and mind. Many people find themselves wanting to fall into a sleepy doze 10 minutes into a session.

For details of where you can find a local practitioner turn to the back of the book to the Useful Addresses section.

65

AN ENERGY ROLLER FOR DIY REFLEXOLOGY AND ACUPRESSURE MASSAGE

TIME: *5–10 minutes, or for as long as you feel comfortable*

INGREDIENTS: *energy roller*

An energy roller is a small wooden device that can be used to massage the feet, the back, face or thighs. Because of its knobbly, spiked surface, when rolled over the body it works on the pressure points and gently releases stresses and tensions.

As with all massage, this simple hand-held tool will increase the supply of oxygen to an area, improving circulation, stimulating energy as blockages and tensions are removed, and generally relaxing as stress is massaged away.

METHOD

1   The instructions couldn't be easier. All you do is roll over the area in need, for five to ten minutes, in order to feel the positive effects. As it is so small, it is portable and can be taken away on business trips, kept in the car or even in a bag or briefcase for when relief is needed.

2   For the feet: according to the principles of reflexology, the foot is a map for the whole body with certain points on the foot mirroring certain parts of the body. If there is crystallization or a blockage at a point on the foot, the corresponding part of the body will also be affected. By applying pressure with the roller, these blocks can be released, which brings relief to the organ the point relates to.

3   For the body: energy (chi) runs through the body along meridian lines, each of which relates to a major organ. As with the points on

the feet, if there are any blocks along these lines, a person's energy levels are affected resulting in stress, fatigue and muscle ache. Use of the roller along the body can help release any blockages, restoring vitality and bringing about a feeling of relaxation and well-being.

An address where you can purchase these rollers is given at the back of the book in the Useful Addresses section.

66

BOOK A REGULAR
AROMATHERAPY SESSION

TIME: *one hour*

INGREDIENTS: *diary, pen, phone*

If you haven't yet discovered the sheer luxury of an aromatherapy massage for relaxation then you're in for a treat. For many people, aromatherapy is a big favourite as not only is it a therapeutic treatment which encourages good health, it is also one of the most pleasurable of all the alternative treatments to receive.

METHOD

1   If you don't have the number of a local practitioner, or a recommendation from anyone you know who's experienced aromatherapy, turn to the back of the book to the Useful Addresses section for organizations which can provide details of aromatherapists in your area.

2   Make an appointment.

An aromatherapy treatment uses a combination of massage and essential oils. There are many different oils used in aromatherapy, each of which has its own unique character, scent and healing property, and also has a psychological as well as a physical effect. They are used for health, to restore balance, encourage the body's own healing power and enhance a feeling of well-being. There are oils that can help just about every ailment there is, but they are particularly useful when it comes to treating stress and any stress-related problems.

Although aromatherapy can help many disorders, it is most effective when used as a preventative treatment. It can stop any complaint from developing from a minor one into a major one, as regular sessions can keep the body relaxed, balanced and in harmony. To many of us in the West, aromatherapy appears to be a relatively new treatment which has become more available nationwide in the last decade. But it is actually an age-old treatment known to the ancient civilizations of Egypt, India, China, Rome, Arabia and Greece.

The oils come from nature, from fruits, flowers, herbs, spices, tree barks, wood and roots. The part that is used in the treatments is the essence of the plant, the part that gives the plant or flower its unique characteristics of colour, scent and shape.

The benefits of the oils are many and varied. All the oils are natural antiseptics and have potent healing properties. Some can be used to relax, others to revive. Good health combines a balance between mind, body and spirit, and aromatherapy is unique as a treatment in that it can work on all these levels relaxing them all. Although the oils can be applied in a variety of ways through compresses, inhalation, in vaporizers and in aromatic baths, a practitioner would apply the oils through massage in an hour's session.

Aromatherapy is a holistic treatment which means the practitioner takes into consideration your whole lifestyle before commencing the first session. A brief medical history plus details of habits, diet and responsibilities will be taken so that the therapist can determine which oils would be best suited to you in your individual circumstances. Once the oils are mixed, all you have to do to is lie back and enjoy the luxurious sensation of the massage with the fragrant healing oils. You will be asked not to shower or bath for six to eight hours after the massage because the oils take that long to be completely absorbed into the system through the skin and blood.

Many people report enjoying the relaxation from the treatment but say that the day after it, they awake feeling particularly refreshed and revitalized, a sensation that can last for a few days after the session.

67

STEP INTO AN AROMATHERAPY STEAM TUBE IN THE COMFORT OF YOUR HOME FOR WARMTH AND RELAXATION

TIME: *10–15 minutes*

INGREDIENTS: *steam tube, lavender oil or alternatives stated below*

The aromatherapy steam tube is a lightweight transparent tube which can be assembled in the home in minutes, so you can enjoy the luxury of a steam bath with essential oils without having to go to a gym or health club.

It measures 66 inches (168 centimetres) high and 36 inches (91.5 centimetres) in diameter and under its floor is a steam generator to which you add water and oils then plug into any domestic electric socket. As the water heats up, steam rises and fills the tube at the temperature required after which you step in, sit down and relax in the heat and fragrant steam.

It is a remarkable invention, not only because of its therapeutic uses but also because it is portable. Once used, it can be dismantled to a height of 16 inches (41 centimetres), perfect for storing or transporting.

METHOD

1   Fill the steam generator at the bottom with water and a relaxing aromatherapy oil such as lavender, rosewood or sandalwood.

2   Set to the desired temperature and wait for it to heat up. (It takes a few minutes to reach the required temperature.)

3   Slide the door open, step in and sit on the stool provided for 15 to

20 minutes, inhaling the therapeutic vapours. There is an adjustable vent in the top of the tube which allows you to control ventilation without moving from the seat.

The penetrating warmth from the steam combined with the healing properties of the oils can be used as a potent aid to help ease muscle tension, aches and pains, fatigue, stress or just generally to relax and unwind.

An address where you can purchase a steam tube is given at the back of the book in the Useful Addresses section.

68

ENJOY A SESSION IN A FLOTATION TANK

TIME: *one hour*

INGREDIENTS: *diary, pen, phone*

This has to be one of the easiest ways available of relaxing, as all you have to do is get in the tank and let your anxieties float away for an hour.

A flotation tank is a huge tub with a lid or roof that is soundproof and lightproof. It is about calf-deep with salinated water which is kept at body temperature in which you can float, usually for about an hour at a time. Many people find it very calming to be in this womb-like environment with an absence of distracting stimuli and they report experiencing states of relaxation similar to those achieved in deep meditation.

METHOD

1 Book in to a health clinic or equivalent venue where they have the tanks. You are usually given a short explanation of what to expect, then given earplugs to keep the water out of your ears and shown a private place where you can leave your clothes when you are in the tank. Some people float naked, others like to float in a swimming costume.

2 Get into the tank which will be lit from the inside and lie down in the water on your back. (The tanks come in different shapes; some are similar to the size of a large sunbed, others are the size of a small room with a door.) Some places provide a sort of rubber support for your neck and head which you can either keep on during your float or remove when you feel that the water is supporting you and you don't need it any more.

3   Once inside, after a few moments, the dim lights are turned off and the tank is completely dark. Some places play gentle music for the first and last five minutes. In the beginning, it is to help you relax, at the end, it is to let you know that the session is almost over, as it is easy to lose all sense of time when you are in there. Most tanks have a dim luminous spot to indicate where the opening is in case you want to get out early.

Although the tank door or lid is shut, it is never locked, so you can get out whenever you want. Some people find the environment initially claustrophobic and like to check that they can get out! It can feel very strange at first to be in a totally dark, silent place. Once this is overcome though and you start to float, the sensation is very relaxing and after a while all you are aware of is your breathing. Some people even fall asleep, others say they can feel the physical stress literally floating away as their body lets go of stiffness and tensions.

Float tanks in centres are always supervised. Although inside you can forget about the outside world and any troubles, there is always someone on the outside who knows that you are in there and will let you know when your time is up.

NB: If you find you relax better to music, take a favourite relaxation tape or music tape, and ask the supervisor or receptionist to put it on so that it will be piped into the tank for you.

For an address of where you can get information about finding a flotation tank centre near you, turn to the back of the book to the Useful Addresses section.

Emotional
Shortcuts

69

A TECHNIQUE FROM KINESIOLOGY FOR EMOTIONAL STRESS RELEASE

TIME: *2–20 minutes*

INGREDIENTS: *chair*

This simple technique is effective for anyone suffering from any kind of anxiety and is instantly calming. It takes 'the sting' out of the worry and helps the person get a lighter perspective on their problem.

METHOD

1 Ask the person who is to be relaxed to sit in a comfortable position.

2 Ask them to close their eyes and concentrate hard on the problem or anxiety that is bothering them. They don't need to verbalize it if they don't want to. Ask them to try and keep focused on one aspect of their distress at a time, even if it starts to diminish. If another layer of stress then emerges, concentrate on that until it also dissipates as you continue with the following technique.

3 Find the points on the forehead immediately above the iris, about halfway between the eyebrows and the person's hairline. Place your fingers on these points with a light pressure.

4 Once you have made contact with the skin, stretch the skin slightly upwards towards the hairline. Maintain this touch with a steady light pressure.

5 For giving added relaxation, use both hands. Touch the two points mentioned above with the thumb and finger of the left hand and cup the back of the head with the right hand. You don't need to use any pressure, the lightest contact is sufficient.

6 Stay like this until the person feels relaxed and the anxiety has diminished. It can take from a few to 20 minutes. When they have got to a point where they can say that their anxiety doesn't seem to matter any more, you know that you have spent sufficient time doing the technique. (Contacting the points on the forehead also stimulates and balances the blood supply to the brain. A healthy blood supply is important for clear thinking.)

NB: You can also do this technique on yourself by making contact with your own forehead.

Kinesiology is a method of rebalancing the systems of the body through muscle testing. Kinesiology comes from the Greek word *kīnēsis*, and means the study of motion. It examines the relationship between the muscles, the lymphatic and vascular systems, and the mechanics of bodily motion.

Although its components are ancient in origin, it was first used in the way we know it now in 1964 by Dr George Goodheart. It claims to be able to help with 80 per cent of the health problems that many people put up with because they're not 'ill' enough to go to the doctor or because they've looked for help but found no relief. Many of these complaints are stress-related. As a result of kinesiology, many people have found that their health and relaxation levels have improved considerably.

70

MAKE TIME TO TALK THROUGH ANXIETIES WITH A FRIEND OR COUNSELLOR

TIME: *30 minutes to an hour*

INGREDIENTS: *a sympathetic friend or relative/counsellor*

You may well be in peak physical shape, exercising and eating a good nutritious diet, but you still can't relax as there's something on your mind. If something's bothering you it's always best to get it out in the open. Often inner stress and anger come about because of a feeling of powerlessness in a situation. You feel you're in an impossible situation and there's no way out. Talking it out can help you find a way to move forward and is a way for you to feel you still have some element of control and can remedy the situation. If anxieties are left unspoken, it only perpetuates the feeling of hopelessness and all the stress that goes with it.

If it's a particular person that you need to talk to about a situation that is causing you stress, anger or sleepless nights, remember the following:

1   Don't let it get out of proportion by winding yourself up for weeks. Make time to relieve the situation before molehills become mountains. Make time to communicate small misunderstandings when they happen, rather than letting them build and eat away at you so that you blast away at the person involved like a tornado with the result that they don't know what's hit them and accuse you of being hysterical or over-dramatizing the situation.

2   Begin by saying something positive so that you don't both start out on the defensive. If you say something good about a person's work or behaviour, they will be much more open to listen to whatever is coming next.

3   When you begin to say what you have to get off your chest, use sentences that start with 'I feel . . .' rather than 'you should', 'you ought to' or 'you did this'. Most people feel under attack if they are blamed for something and will counterattack and be defensive: the next thing you know you're in a no-win situation.

4   Take responsibility for your part in it all.

5   Listen and consider what the other person has to say and feed back what they have said to you in your own words, so that they feel that you have really heard what they've said. (Hopefully they will do the same for you.)

6   Say everything you need to, even if this means going into the situation with a list of points as you would for a business meeting. Often if the circumstance is emotionally charged, it is easy to forget what you need to say in the heat of the moment. A prepared list will help you keep on track.

If it's a temporary crisis at work, a relationship problem or a more long-term anxiety that is causing you stress, and you feel that you can't talk to the person involved, often the best solution is to talk matters through with a friend or relative. If ignored, emotional feelings can build and result in physical symptoms such as headaches, insomnia, irritability, constipation and stress. Anxieties can be relieved by simply talking to a sympathetic ear, but if you haven't got anybody that you feel you can sort things through with, you can always seek the help of a counsellor.

Counselling isn't only for the sick or mentally ill but also for people who need help riding a crisis, who want to improve some aspect of their life or feel they have exhausted the sympathy of friends and relatives. If you feel that you've become like a record that's got stuck over a particular problem – divorce, separation, a recent loss or death, redundancy, finances – and feel that people think you ought to be over it by now, whatever your problem is, it might help to get some counselling. The good thing about seeing a counsellor is that you can talk freely to a neutral and uninvolved person who won't contradict or interrupt and who won't force you to talk about something you're not ready to.

The last thing you need when you are feeling stressed is for someone to say, 'oh cheer up, things could be worse', or 'OK, enough about you, what about me? Now *my* problems really are bad.'

Counsellors are trained to help you to talk freely which can be extremely beneficial as it can help you clarify your situation yourself. If you don't like a particular counsellor, find another one: it is important that you feel you can open up to whoever you're talking to. Some counsellors have specific training to deal with marital problems, addictions, bereavement, career problems, abuse and so on.

Alternatively, for someone uninvolved to listen to you, you can also go to a priest, a doctor or a rabbi.

For addresses of where you can find a local counsellor, turn to the Useful Addresses section at the back of the book.

71

A TECHNIQUE FOR RELEASING ANGER AND FRUSTRATION

TIME: *5–10 minutes, or however long you need*

INGREDIENTS: *cushion or chair*

This is the perfect technique to release any anger or frustration that you may be feeling towards someone but can't express. Sometimes it's just not appropriate to show it: for example, you can't yell at your boss no matter how much he/she has angered you; or perhaps you can't say what you really feel to a loved one or friend for fear of hurting them, or perhaps the person who has upset you has moved or even passed away. In the meantime, feelings get all bottled up inside you, gnawing away and causing stress, anger or frustration. All negative emotions are always better out than in so try the following technique.

METHOD

1 Find a room or place where you will be undisturbed and where you know you can be as noisy as you like without frightening the neighbours!

2 Choose a cushion or chair to represent whoever it is that you need to speak to: your boss, your lover, your spouse, your child, your parent, your neighbour, God.

3 Place the cushion opposite you and begin to say what you need to. If it helps, close your eyes to visualize them in the spot where your cushion is. You might start out being rational or you may jump right in being angry; whichever, but give yourself permission to really let rip. No one is standing in judgement here or going to hold anything you say against you.

To begin with you may feel foolish but continue and you will find that before long, it all comes spilling out. Let go. You can really get it off your chest. Yell, scream, swear, stomp your feet, make no sense if that's how it comes out. Say all the hurtful things that you don't dare to say to their face. If you feel like it, kick the cushion, throw it about, jump on it. Be enraged. Get it all out until you feel all you needed to say has been said.

4 Once you have said your bit, swop places. Go and stand where you placed your cushion to represent the person. Close your eyes and reply to what you just said from their position. When they have had their say (through you), go back to your original place and see if you want to reply again.

5 Go back and forth until you sense that all that needed to be said has been said.

You may be surprised at how you feel in the end. Many people feel energized, as if a dam has burst. Some feel tired but relieved; others feel like crying. You may have unearthed deeper feelings for the person represented, such as compassion, forgiveness or love. You may still feel angry. But in every case, the energy it has taken holding it all in is now freed and the overall feeling is of relaxation, relief to have got it out. There is also the fact that you have safely released your feelings rather than leaving them to explode in real life.

If you feel you cannot cope with the excess of emotion tapped into then you may benefit by booking some sessions with a qualified practitioner to go into it on a deeper level. But in the meantime, this simple method works for most people who can't express themselves in the actual situation.

72

LET OFF STEAM BY WRITING A LETTER THEN THROW IT AWAY

TIME: *as long as you like (it depends on what you have to say)*

INGREDIENTS: *paper, pen*

As with the previous step, this is a way of letting off steam and getting out any frustration or unresolved emotions that for whatever reason you cannot express to someone's face. Maybe it is inappropriate, maybe you aren't sure what you want to say, but something's bugging you and you can't let it go.

Here's your chance to get it out without feeling it has to come out right first time, or that you are going to be judged. You can spend time on a letter and rewrite and rewrite until you are happy with your result. No one's going to see what you've written because you are doing this for you so that you can have your say and move on.

METHOD

1 Simply get a wad of note paper and a pen and start writing. Dear —

2 Get it all out. Be angry, swear, call them names if that's how you feel. Or maybe it's to do with an unresolved problem from a relationship. Express what you felt. How hurt you were. What you went through. What you are still going through. Write it all down. Put it all in. Even if it takes you days to write (the chances are you will finish one bit then hours later think, 'oh, and another thing'). Go and add whatever else comes to mind – no matter how unreasonable, sloppy, horrible or sentimental.

3 When you feel you've got it all out, destroy it. Some people like to burn these letters. Others like to rip them up dramatically then throw them away. Do whatever feels best for you.

In the old days, it was called letting off steam or getting it off your chest and can work to enable you to move on to a clearer future, having had your say about the past.

73

EXPRESS ANXIETIES THROUGH PAINTING AND DRAWING

TIME: *15 minutes to an hour*

INGREDIENTS: *(depending on which medium you prefer) – paint, paper, brushes, crayons, charcoal, pencils, water or clay, table*

Art can be an excellent release for stress, particularly for those who feel that they can't communicate their anxiety through talking because their feelings aren't identifiable in words or are so deep that they are difficult to bring to the surface. The important thing about anxiety of any sort is that it is better expressed and out than kept in causing depression, fatigue and stress.

Using art as a release for stress is not like taking it up as a hobby or to do 'nice' or technically good pictures. The idea is to use art materials as a means to release deep-seated emotions and anxieties that are debilitating.

METHOD

1   Prepare your work surface and materials. You can use charcoal, pencil, paint or clay – whichever appeals most at the time. Have plenty of paper to hand.

2   To begin with, do a series of fast two- to five-minute sketches. Focus on how you are feeling and, using as many sheets as you want, paint, draw or scribble. What you do can be figurative or abstract or both.

Give your feelings a shape. Big, small, round, jagged, whatever. Give your feelings a colour. Give yourself permission to make a mess if you want. You don't need to be good at art for this, it is just for you. No one need see what you do and you can throw away your papers when you've finished if you don't want to keep them. Just use the materials to get out whatever feelings you want to express. You may even surprise yourself by what comes up.

3 After your series of short sketches, take 10 to 15 minutes to do a longer one. Again focus on how you're feeling. Has someone intimidated you? Draw them in, real or abstract. Are they large, small, black, with a huge head and nasty expression? Let it out, however you feel. Put your reason on hold along with the old training of trying to make it look nice. Let rip. Where are you in the picture? Put yourself in if you want. Or on the other hand you may just want to slosh paint on in a whole soup of colour because that's exactly how you feel – mixed up!

4 Do a longer piece of work. Again, it doesn't have to be realistic or 'good'. Slash away with your brush if you're feeling angry. Paint over situations or people if it feels good. Distort. Whatever you feel like but keep focused on the feelings you want out and see what happens.

Afterwards, you may not want to keep any of the papers; in fact, some people find it therapeutic to destroy them and throw them away as though disposing of the negativity they've felt. Or you may like to keep them as a reminder of how you felt.

You may even find that you've created a work of art full of colour, passion and intensity and that you want to keep it, but the real object of the exercise is getting feelings out on paper to make you feel freer, lighter and more relaxed – not to produce great works of art.

There are also other forms of creative work that you can do to release feelings.

Music therapy Just as music can evoke emotional responses, it can also release emotions. Use musical instruments in the same ways that you use the art materials to express how you feel. Bang out your emotion on a drum, thrash it out on a guitar, or keyboards, or a xylophone.

Dance therapy Dance was used in many cultures long ago to help release feelings bad and good and sadly this has largely disappeared in this day and age. In ancient Egypt, the women of the court all used to come together and do a trance dance of growing intensity to help anyone who was feeling negative disperse their feelings. They'd fling out feelings through flaying arms, a building fervour of motion and a fast whirling of total letting go.

Dancing at home or attending dance classes can be an excellent way of releasing emotion as well as good exercise.

Drama therapy You can act out stressful situations by giving them to a character in a play and working in a situation tailor-made for stress release which, while acceptable on a stage, may not be appropriate in everyday circumstances.

Addresses of places where all these therapies can be done under the guidance of a trained therapist are at the back of the book in the Useful Addresses section. However, you can also help yourself by simply letting rip at home, dancing, playing an instrument or painting to your heart's content.

74

A STOMPING EXERCISE TO LET ANGER OUT

TIME: *5–10 minutes*

INGREDIENTS: *chair*

This is an excellent exercise to release anger. You may feel a bit foolish doing it, but persevere. Afterwards you'll feel better for it, even if it is only that, in the end, it made you laugh so much you forgot what bothered you in the first place.

Before you start, either tell others in your house what you're doing as they may think you've gone slightly mad or wait until you're on your own in the house and you can make as much noise as you like without feeling inhibited.

METHOD

1   Sit in a chair with your feet firmly on the ground. Rest your forearms on your thighs, with your palms facing upwards. Close your eyes.

2   Begin to gently tap the backs of your hands on your thighs whilst focusing on the object of your anger. Let whatever feelings you have come up.

3   Start to make noises of anger. Grunt right from the pit of your stomach. As you do, make your tapping on the thighs harder, firmer and more purposeful. Continue grunting and tapping hard for a few moments.

4   Open your eyes and stand up. Clench your fists and bend your elbows and lift your hands up to shoulder-level.

5 Focus in again on whatever or whoever has made you angry. Start to grunt your objections louder and louder. As you do, slam your hands down to your side, straightening your arms with a sweeping hard movement. At the same time, bend one knee up and bring it down hard to the floor. Synchronize the two movements so that it feels like you are breaking a stick across your thighs. A firm strong stomp.

6 Repeat with the other leg.

7 Repeat again and again, grunting and stomping about until all of your anger has gone.

75

HAVE A GOOD SCREAM!

TIME: *5 minutes, or for as long as you feel like*

INGREDIENTS: *Pillow or cushion*

This is for when you feel uptight, frustrated, wound-up, and about to shout someone's (anyone's) head off.

The car won't start and you're late for work. You've just had a row with your wife/husband/partner/child. Your overdraft is being called in. The trains are on strike. The pressure's on at the office. There's just been another bomb. And it's raining. What you need now isn't a vitamin B complex or a massage. It's a good scream.

So many days, we push down frustration, anger, irritation from the major to the minor just to get by. And how does it affect us? Stress. So let it all out.

If you feel self-conscious or stupid, wait until there's no one around, or close all the doors and turn up some music then begin.

METHOD

1 Open wide and scream. If any words or angry thoughts come up, say them out aloud as fast and ear-splittingly loud as you can. Yell them. If you only think them, they'll slip back into the unconscious. If you let them out they'll be gone. So let rip, use bad language, swear.

If you really think you may be overheard and this inhibits you howl into a big pillow or cushion. If it feels feeble and weak to start with, give yourself permission to let go. Scream from the pit of your stomach and continue until it's all out. Keep trying for a few moments until you're off and squealing like a two-year-old.

Scream about the government, your work, the bank, finances, relationships, the weather, strikes, terrorism, all the annoying factors that anger or irritate you but which you can't control.

You may like to add movement. Have a cushion handy, kick it and stomp on it if you feel like it. Have a full-blown tantrum. Learn from kids, they know how to let off steam. And how. Nothing held back. Then it's all over and forgotten. Not us adults, we carry it round for weeks getting headaches, biting people's heads off, taking it out on those close to us, getting neck ache and not sleeping.

2   Lie on the bed and thrash your arms and legs about. You may feel a bit mad doing it but who cares? No one's watching. And it works. You'll feel energized and surprisingly more relaxed afterwards.

76

HAVE A GOOD LAUGH REGULARLY

TIME: *at least 10–30 minutes weekly*

INGREDIENTS: *local paper, videos, tapes, TV or books*

Seriously . . . How often do we hear that laughter is the best medicine or laughter is good for the soul? It's true. A good weekly dose of laughter can do wonders for maintaining a healthy perspective and balanced outlook as well as being one of the most pleasurable ways of releasing stress. Most humour is derived from pain as comedians point out the absurdities of life, the struggles we're all up against and make observations about some of the people we exist alongside – the government, relatives, celebrities. We can laugh in recognition and realize we're not alone, everybody's just trying to get by and stay sane in a world of change and contradictions. Sometimes it's just good to sit back, forget the fight for a few hours and laugh at our predicament.

METHOD

Check out:

1 local video shops for your favourite film and TV shows;

2 local clubs and pubs for live comedy shows;

3 newspapers for nationwide tours of all-time favourite comedians and shows;

4 TV listings for sit-coms, comedy drama, entertainment programmes;

5 cassette tapes for the car. Being stuck in traffic when listening to a humorous tape can keep you amused instead of wound-up;

6 books – novels or joke books.

Environmental
Shortcuts

77

GET AN AIR IONIZER FOR A ROOM OF MOUNTAIN-PURE AIR

TIME: *just as long as it takes to plug in*

INGREDIENTS: *ionizer*

An ionizer is a small device that creates an ionization zone by emitting a stream of negative ions (known as the vitamins of the air). It can be plugged in at home or in the office and gives the feeling of freshness that we can only usually experience in the country, mountains or at the seaside, where there are usually 1,000 to 2,000 ions per cubic centimetre. This is in contrast to the city where there are frequently fewer than 100 ions per cubic centimetre.

Ions are electrically charged molecules that exist in the air around us and which we subsequently breathe in. Some ions are positively charged, others negatively. It is the negatively charged ions that are so predominant in the pure air outside the city and which generally give us the sensation of clean, fresh air that makes us feel so good. However, it is also the negative ions that are affected adversely by factors such as pollution and dust; they can be trapped in a smoky room or by a television screen or in heating systems. This can leave an imbalance in the atmosphere as the positive ions then begin to dominate and it is these that can leave people feeling depressed or listless. For example, the effects of a predominance of positive ions can be felt just prior to a thunderstorm or in a particularly smoky, overheated room when the usual reaction is for people to feel stifled or restless.

Although some people don't seem to be affected at all by changes in ionization, there are others who are more susceptible and suffer because of it. A decrease in the negative ions present in the air can result in headaches, allergic reactions, stress and mood changes.

As well as emitting ions, an ionizer cleans the air of dust, pollen and bacteria and has been known to help alleviate asthma, hay fever and other respiratory problems aggravated by airborne allergies.

They cost around £50 and most are guaranteed for five years. So that's £10 a year for pure clear air. They are available from most good health shops.

78

WAKE UP WITH A NATURAL ALARM CLOCK (FOR A SPRING DAY IN THE MIDDLE OF WINTER)

TIME: *15–45 minutes*

INGREDIENTS: *natural alarm clock*

If you are someone who finds it hard to get out of bed in winter and who dreads waking up on those dark, drab mornings, you can get a wake-up call from a natural alarm clock which simulates the light of a gently breaking dawn.

During the night, the pineal gland produces a substance called melatonin which makes us drowsy. At daybreak, the bright light from the dawn causes the gland to stop producing melatonin and so we wake up. However, on a dark day, especially if you have an early call, there is not enough light to trigger this waking up process. The natural alarm clock can remedy this.

In the morning, about half an hour before your set time, the lamp at the top of the clock begins to glow, faintly at first, then gradually increasing in intensity until it reaches full when a normal alarm beeper sounds. You can press the control at any time to prevent the beeper sounding and to adjust the light level. On a dull dreary winter morning, it is a natural and cheerful way to wake up, especially when you know that it's miserable or raining outside.

Plants aren't the only living organisms that need sunlight. Human beings do too and being deprived of it affects many people more than they realize. Just as plants don't thrive and grow when starved of sunlight, in the same way, humans can literally feel themselves wilting in offices where the only lighting is artificial, or in winter when sunlight is at its minimum. Atmospheric pollution in cities also interferes with the quality of light.

Some people are more affected by a lack of bright light than others (the condition is called SAD – seasonal affective disorder). But for all of us, the lack of light, especially in winter, can result in nervous fatigue, concentration lapses, depression, mood swings and irritability, which goes some way to explaining why people feel so lousy after a season indoors in unnatural conditions. Contrary to popular thought on light therapy, the full spectrum lightbulbs you can buy are not sufficient to remedy SAD, nor is trying to increase the wattage. The light must be very bright (at least five times brighter than normal office lighting); it must also be safe to use with the harmful ultraviolet part of the spectrum filtered out.

The safest and most effective treatment is to get a light box from a specialist in light-therapy treatments. The box emits a level of white light similar to a bright spring morning: the idea is to sit in front of it for 15 to 45 minutes a day as the light similar to daylight fills the room with its bright glow. You don't have to stare at the light box, you can go about normal activities, reading or watching TV. Just ensure that the light from the box is reaching the eyes.

For more information and details of the full range of light boxes and where you can buy them or a natural alarm clock, an address is given at the back of the book in the Useful Addresses section.

79

CARRY EARPLUGS

TIME: *as long as you sleep*

INGREDIENTS: *earplugs*

This method has to be the simplest and is certainly the cheapest of the environmental approaches. It doesn't so much change the environment as cut it out when you need a bit of peace and quiet, either at home or when travelling. It is an invaluable shortcut to relaxation in a variety of sometimes unpredictable and unforeseen situations where you need to rest but are disturbed by numerous sounds that can interrupt sleep. These situations might include:

1 Staying somewhere unfamiliar, for example, a hotel, a friend's house or a B and B – you can never predict the noise levels and may get landed in a room with roaring air conditioning (or even worse, next to the air conditioning generator); roaring traffic outside your window, loud neighbours, creaking floorboards; all sorts of unfamiliar sounds that can disturb the pattern of sleep. The last thing you need if it's the first day of your holiday or if you have a business meeting is to stagger out in the morning bleary-eyed and worn out because of interrupted sleep. Earplugs can simply cut out the disturbing element of noise and allow you to sleep in peace.

2 Sleeping in a property with rowdy neighbours who come in late, or neighbours with young children, or dogs who wake at the break of dawn.

3 Aeroplane or train journeys where you want to close off and get a bit of sleep without the incessant roar of the engines in your ears.

4 Sleeping with a partner who snores.

METHOD

1 Don't wait until you need them. Where are you going to get a pair of earplugs at 3am in a strange hotel? Keep them handy by purchasing them in advance and always carrying them for use when the occasion rises.

2 When needed, simply get them out and insert them into your ears.

Earplugs come in two types of material, either wax or sponge, and are available from most chemists. Both types can be rolled with the fingertips into a small shape and should be inserted into both ears where the wax or sponge will adapt itself to the shape of your ear. If you have an alarm call or phone call to wake you, you will still hear the sound if the phone or clock is close to your head. It is the sounds that are further away that will be screened out allowing you to sleep in peace.

80

INVEST IN AN ADJUSTABLE BED

TIME: *once in place, all you have to do is enjoy*

INGREDIENTS: *adjustable bed*

For those who like their relaxation time to be totally undemanding, buy an adjustable bed. It will adapt to your needs at the touch of a button, either raising the top or the bottom depending on your requirement.

Bed is where people spend a lot of time, either sleeping, snoozing, reading or watching TV, so it makes sense to invest in one that can support different positions without having to resort to propping yourself up with loads of pillows.

Gone are the days when beds were all flat and immobile. Now you can buy a bed that can be adjusted to meet changing needs and positions whilst providing comfort and support.

Most adjustable beds give you five options:

1 Seated, which is excellent for reading or watching TV in bed or for those who need help in getting in and out of bed.

2 The head raised slightly, which is beneficial for anyone with breathing problems, hay fever, sinusitis, bronchitis or heart problems.

3 Contour sleeping which is slightly raised at the top and bottom. This kind of support is good for anyone suffering from arthritic aches and pain.

4 Feet up to help circulation, varicose veins or swollen legs or ankles.

5 Flat for those who prefer to sleep flat.

For details of where you can purchase such a bed see the Useful Addresses section at the back of the book.

81

CHANGE YOUR PILLOW
FOR AN ORTHOPAEDIC ONE

TIME: *once you've bought it, no more effort is required apart from sleeping on it*

INGREDIENTS: *orthopaedic pillow*

Sleeping on an orthopaedically designed pillow supports your head in a good position and can relieve back and neck ache as well as help you get a better night's sleep. If you have been sleeping with a pillow that is too hard or too soft, back strain or neck ache due to awkward positioning in the night can be a result.

A whole range of orthopaedic pillows are available now, offering a variety of thickness and softness. Some even have two sides to suit different people's preferences: they have a soft side and a firm side so you can choose by simply turning the pillow over, but both support the head and neck ensuring a good night's sleep without ending up in an uncomfortable position.

Many orthopaedic pillows are also designed to be allergy-free: the material used in some standard pillows can break down in time to produce dust and so attract microscopic dust mites that can cause allergic reactions, sore eyes being one of them.

Most major department stores keep them but if you have difficulty getting one, there are addresses at the back of the book in the Useful Addresses section where you can purchase them by mail order.

82

GET AN ANSWERING MACHINE

TIME: *for use whenever you want*

INGREDIENTS: *the answering machine*

An answering machine is an excellent addition to your household if you have decided to take your relaxation time seriously.

They aren't just for putting on when you are out but are also for use when you are home or in your office but want some quiet time without interruption. Often people say, 'oh, I don't need one, I'm always at home' or 'I'm always in the office'. Precisely. Always available means no time for privacy or true relaxation. Everyone needs time off occasionally from the invasion of telephone calls, time to have a proper break for lunch or five minutes to read the papers. With the addition of an answering machine to your home, you can screen your calls and answer at your own convenience.

TIMES WHEN AN ANSWERING MACHINE COULD BE USEFUL

- Watching a movie and it's just got to the climax of the whole film (the last thing you want is the phone to ring)
- Cooking for family or guests
- You're in a hurry, you're late and have to get out of the house quickly
- You want to have a lie-in
- You're in the bath
- Having friends over
- You're meditating
- Having a massage
- Just unwinding generally after a stressful or demanding day
- You're waiting for a call but need to pop out for a short time

- You're in a meeting or with someone to whom you want to give your whole attention
- simply tired out and don't want to talk to another soul for half an hour

You will still get your messages if anyone needs to get hold of you. The advantage of this useful machine is that it allows you to pace yourself to suit yourself, rather than being at the beck and call of everyone who rings you.

METHOD

1 Purchase your machine. They are available at most shops that sell electrical equipment and come in all sizes, some with built-in phones or fax machines.

2 Plug it in and connect it to your phone as directed in the simple instructions that come with it. There you have it, an easy shortcut to peace and relaxation at the turn of a switch.

83

SIT COMFORTABLY, PREVENT AND RELIEVE BACKACHE WITH A CHAIR DESIGNED TO CORRECT BAD POSTURE

TIME: *for use whenever you're at your desk, dining table or doing table work*

INGREDIENTS: *specially designed chair*

There are a variety of chairs now available that have been designed for maximum comfort but that also help you to sit correctly, preventing the strain and backache that can result from bad posture.

Some of the chairs are designed for desk work, others for at home when you relax, but all have been devised to help you sit in a more comfortable and natural position as well as prevent slumping and bad posture.

As someone who works at a computer most of the day, I am well aware of the strain that awkward posture can make on the back. One example of the chairs that I came across that particularly impressed me is called a wave stool. It was comfortable to sit on and immediately I found myself sitting straight but without any force or strain. It has a large round top which allows your legs to fall out slightly at the knees. (This is the most relaxed position for the legs but is one that most chairs with square bases interfere with.)

Built on rockers, it encourages natural balance. These rockers allow the seat angle to adjust exactly to your individual height so that you can sit comfortably for longer. By simply moving back or forward, you cause the angle to vary to where you need support. Also, because of the rockers, whenever you move back or forward, the stool moves with you, always providing support. The rockers also help you stand up correctly. You rock forward onto your feet and up in one smooth movement. This is a method of standing that can prevent further back strain.

The stool allows you to put your feet where you like, unlike the designs of some of the other support chairs which, although good for posture, can restrict your position.

As much of our time is spent either sitting working at desks or computers, or sitting reading or watching TV, the design of what we sit on is important for a stress-free back and neck. It's only too easy to get into unhealthy sitting positions as we get involved in whatever we're doing, then feel the effects of a tight neck or aching lower back later. Some positions that people sit in can distort the lower spine, cause back strain or even injury. Improving sitting habits can prevent any damage from happening as well as providing a comfortable chair to sit on.

The wave stool has been developed by a furniture maker who has been studying the Alexander technique since 1988. He has incorporated his understanding of the technique in the making of the stool.

All the chairs designed for correct sitting come in different styles and different sizes for different heights. An address where you can write for further details about the wave stool, or for brochures of chairs, is given at the back in the Useful Addresses section.

84

INVEST IN A JACUZZI IN THE BATHROOM

TIME: *once installed, you can use it whenever and for however long you wish*

INGREDIENTS: *jacuzzi bath, relaxing aromatherapy oils as stated below*

For the ultimate in relaxation have an aqua massage in the comfort of your own home.

Warm air is simply pumped into the bath water through hundreds of air jets in the bottom or side of the bath. These tiny air bubbles have a deep pulsating action that massages the body, gently easing away tension and stress and so providing a wonderful all-over body massage. The after-effect is not only restorative and relaxing but also offers relief from lower back pain, muscular aches, rheumatic and arthritic stiffness.

The benefits of bathing in warm water have been well known since Greek and Roman times and it is the combination of the heated water and aqua massage that makes a jacuzzi such a luxurious experience. These baths were first inspired by nature after an inventor watched the air bubbles at a waterfall and decided to create a similar effect, turning the air bubble action of water into a therapeutic experience. For many years, these baths were used exclusively for hydrotherapy in sports clinics, hospitals and health spas, but nowadays most good bathroom shops are able to supply them so that you can indulge yourself in the comfort of your own home.

NB: For increased relaxation, add three drops of essential oil of rosemary (good for muscular aches and pains) and three drops of lavender (excellent for unwinding and enhancing relaxation after a long day).

85

PURCHASE AN AUDIO CASSETTE FOR RELAXATION

TIME: *usually between 30 and 60 minutes*

INGREDIENTS: *audio casette, tape recorder*

If you are someone who responds well to sound, music and suggestion, one of the many relaxation tapes on the market these days may work well for you as an aid to unwinding – all you have to do is switch on and drift away.

The tapes for relaxation fall into three main areas:

1 Music tapes to calm and soothe. These consist purely of tranquil music (usually instrumental) that has been composed especially with relaxation in mind. They use pleasant melodic sounds that are non-intrusive, often with lots of strings, piano, flute or harp. They are very easy on the ear, and it is a pleasant way to drift away into a state of gentle relaxation.

2 Sounds of nature tapes: these generally consist of instrumental compositions mixed with sounds of the rainforest or the sea – waves breaking at the ocean, birds singing, the sounds of whales' and dolphins' voices.

3 Self-change programming tapes: subliminal suggestions. The tapes cover areas such as how to achieve a calm and peaceful mind, how to sleep well, how to control stress in general.

Most of the tapes consist of relaxing music behind which is a voice, mixed in so that you don't consciously hear it. This voice makes suggestions to your unconscious mind according to whichever tape you have chosen. The theory is that as the ideas are accepted by the unconscious, you will begin to make changes in your conscious life to alter it in accordance. For example, if the tape were concerned with sleeping better, the subliminal proposals would be something like: you will sleep peacefully through the night; when you lie down you will fall into a very deep and refreshing sleep. When you awake you will feel revitalized, restored. You can sleep when you want to and so on.

The tapes are available in some health shops around the country but if you have difficulty finding one, there are details in the Useful Addresses section at the back of the book of places which sell them by mail order. If you send for a catalogue you will see the full range of tapes available.

86

LEARN ABOUT FENG SHUI OR HAVE A PRACTITIONER VISIT YOUR HOME TO HELP CREATE A HARMONIOUS ENVIRONMENT

TIME: *varies, depending on the size of your property*

INGREDIENTS: *Feng Shui book or practitioner*

WHAT FENG SHUI IS

It is the art of arranging homes and workplaces as well as the design features, furniture and objects within them to create a harmonious, energizing and supportive living and working environment. It has been practised in the Orient for at least 3,000 years, although its philosophies date back to an even earlier period.

Its fundamental desire is to acknowledge the power of the natural world and work in accordance and harmony with this. If as a race we ignore the natural forces, it can affect us both ecologically (e.g. the widespread felling of trees and the redirection of rivers can lead to drought and floods) and environmentally (disharmony or blocks to the life force in the home can lead to stress, fatigue, minor ailments and a general sense of things not feeling right).

Feng Shui experts believe that just as the life force (or chi) must flow freely through the body for health and well-being, in the same way benevolent forces must be able to flow freely through our living and working environment for us to be able to function and live to our maximum potential in harmony and without stress. If there are blocks in the body, health will suffer. If there are blocks in the environment, the atmosphere that we live and work in can affect our well-being, energy levels and, inevitably, our state of health.

The philosophy of Feng Shui would explain why some places have a feel that is welcoming and relaxing whereas other places feel uncomfortable or make you feel ill at ease. Feng Shui experts believe that creating the ideal home goes much deeper than interior design and picking the right colours, fabrics and curtains. Just as the saying 'beauty comes from within' suggests that beauty can't be painted on with make-up or clothing, so with a house or office, attention must be made to deeper factors that concern the balancing of natural forces with the environment – the relationship of a place to its surroundings or the implications of the way in which a building is orientated.

FENG SHUI IN PRACTICE

As each house or building is completely unique, recommendations are individual and specific. A Feng Shui practitioner would have to visit your home or at least have details of the inhabitants, location and site with floor plans before giving advice. Rather like a surveyor's visit when buying a house, a Feng Shui practitioner would take into consideration all the details pertaining to the property – date of the building, decor, placement of furniture, doors, mirrors as well as birth dates of all the household members. From these notes and his observations, he would prepare a report with recommendations for change that would enhance your home or office and create a more energizing and peaceful environment.

Alternatively, you can attend workshops or study books on the subject and learn how to apply this art yourself. An address and phone number are given at the back of the book in the Useful Addresses section, where you can get more information about practitioners or classes near you.

87

USE COLOUR TO CHANGE MOOD

TIME: *15 minutes*

From as far back as the ancient Egyptians, colour has been believed to have a powerful effect on us as a healing agent. It can bring feelings of calm or it can arouse. Sayings we are all familiar with, such as 'he's feeling off colour', 'she's feeling blue', 'he was green with envy', 'I saw red', suggest that colour images do influence us more than we consciously realize.

Read the following guide to see how each colour is said to affect us. Depending on your different needs at different times, you can consciously dress or surround yourself with the colour you feel will benefit you the most. Or you can take it a stage further and use colour to create an atmosphere that is calming or energizing when decorating your home.

THE COLOURS

Red is stimulating, it represents passion, energy and aggression. To dress in red is good for someone who has been depressed or deeply fatigued.

Orange is revitalizing and energizing. It is beneficial for anyone lacking in confidence or who has been suffering from nervous complaints.

Yellow is cleansing and mentally stimulating. It is good for sluggishness and promotes happiness. It is useful for anyone needing to concentrate a lot – for example, preparing for exams or a presentation.

Green is peaceful and brings balance and harmony. It acts as a tonic to the system and is good for anyone who is stressed or over-emotional.

Blue is soothing and healing. It helps bring about peace of mind and acceptance, induces relaxation and can also help in reducing fever.

Indigo is calming and purifying. It is the colour used by people who want to develop their psychic abilities and is also good for anyone who is feeling emotionally unstable.

Violet is harmonizing. It is used to help any mental or nervous complaints and is the colour of spiritual awareness.

Pink is the colour of warmth and love and is often used as a healing colour.

Apricot is soft and relaxing. It is good for physical and emotional exhaustion.

88

GET A PET

TIME: *owning a pet is a full-time commitment*

INGREDIENTS: *dog, cat, bird or whatever you choose!*

The benefits of owning a pet are now starting to be recognized as an aid to relaxation, not only because animals make excellent companions but also because the act of stroking and grooming, for example, dogs and cats lowers the heart rate, lowers blood pressure and reduces stress. The Royal Society of Medicine published a study in 1991 confirming that 71 per cent of people acquiring pets said that minor health complaints had improved, and there were benefits which lasted long after the initial new attraction of ownership had passed.

A society called Pets As Therapy is now so popular that it finds it difficult to keep up with demand. Dogs and their owners visit hospices and are actually prescribed to help some people who are withdrawn, phobic and unhappy, as dogs can sometimes break through the loneliness barrier.

The benefits of owning a pet are:

1   At least for dog owners, overall improved physical health as they take walks that they probably wouldn't take without the dog. Dogs have to be taken out every day ensuring that their owners also get plenty of fresh air and exercise.

2   Friendship. If treated well, cats and dogs reward their owners by being loyal and affectionate. The act of stroking and grooming gives pleasure to both animal and owner, and you can always expect an enthusiastic welcome home (especially if around their dinner time!).

3   In a time of increasing housebreaks, dogs act as added security, scaring off intruders and letting you know if there is anyone approaching the house or trying to get in. This can only result in people feeling safer and more relaxed, especially if they live alone.

4 Walking a dog helps break the ice with other people and can help lonely people make a natural and spontaneous contact with others.

5 Watching a cat or dog's antics can entertain and relax. Being uninvolved in the everyday problems so many of us carry about, they can help us forget our cares for a while. And if you want to learn how to relax, watch cats. They are masters of serenity.

NB: Acquiring a pet must be as much for the animal's sake as for you. In providing yourself with a companion that can give unconditional friendship, in turn you must be able to provide a good home and the time to look after them. As the saying goes, a dog is for life, not just for Christmas. However, that life can be much enhanced by the presence of a devoted furry friend.

If you would like to find out more about the organization Pets As Therapy, there is an address at the back of the book in the Useful Addresses section.

Spiritual Shortcuts

89

BURN FRANKINCENSE OIL

TIME: *5–20 minutes*

INGREDIENTS: *essential oil of frankincense, an oil burner pot, water, a night-light candle*

It is no coincidence that frankincense has been burnt on the altars of churches and temples since ancient times, nor that it was one of the gifts taken by the Magi to the infant Jesus to celebrate his birth. Frankincense was one of the most precious and sought-after commodities in ancient times. It was used by high priests in ancient Egypt partly because of its physical healing properties but also because of its uplifting effect on the emotions. As well as using frankincense in rituals and ceremonies (it was offered to the Sun god), they would inhale the aroma of the burning frankincense while meditating, to encourage spiritual awareness, expand their consciousness and develop psychic abilities.

Nowadays we know that one of the properties of frankincense oil is its ability to slow down and deepen the breathing, so producing a calm effect that the priests would have found conducive to prayer and meditation. German scientists researching the oil in the 1980s found that a psychoactive substance is produced when the gum is burnt.

The oil is derived from the resin of the bark of trees (Boswellia serrata and Boswellia carteri) grown in Africa in Ethiopia, Lebanon, Somalia, and in China and southern Arabia. It is extracted from the resin of the bark by steam distillation and is used today for various ailments: nervous conditions, stress, tension, respiratory complaints (particularly asthma which is often rooted in anxiety – the frankincense helps ease breathing and calms the emotions). It is also good for skin care and can help reduce wrinkles.

I have put it first in the section of spiritual approaches to relaxation so that you have a choice. You can burn it for its evocative and uplifting scent as well as to help you slow down your breathing and feel calmer. But you also have the option of using the oil in conjunction with other shortcuts to help induce a peaceful frame of mind in which to try any of the later techniques of meditation and prayer.

METHOD

1 Place six to eight drops of frankincense oil in a tablespoonful of water in the top of your oil burner. (The burner, or vaporizer, was described in shortcut 54 in the alternative remedy section and can be purchased at some health shops but can also be obtained from the supplier of aromatherapy oils listed at the back in the Useful Addresses section.) The pottery burners have two levels. The top one is to put the oil and water in.

2 Light your night-light candle and place it on the lower level. The night-light will warm the top level and the oil, causing the aroma of frankincense to fill the atmosphere. As the oil is breathed in through the lungs it will enter the system through the blood-stream and start to do its work, calming the emotions and slowing the breath. All you have to do is inhale the aroma as the Egyptian high priests did so many centuries ago.

Alternative ways of vaporizing a room with frankincense are:
a) Wet a small towel, wring it out and sprinkle six to eight drops of frankincense oil onto it, then place the towel on a hot radiator. As the towel dries, the scent of frankincense will permeate the atmosphere.
b) Put six to eight drops of the frankincense oil into a bowl of steaming water. As the oil hits the hot water and steam, it will release its scent.
c) Stir the frankincense oil into a bowl of pot pourri. This is a particular favourite around Christmas when the warmer, spicier scents are popular. You could mix it with orange, myrrh and cinnamon for a really seasonal fragrance.

The three methods mentioned above will release the scent of the oil into the room for only a short while. The advantage of the pot burner is that as the night-light burns, the scent of the oil tends to last and permeate a room for much longer. Also, you can easily keep topping up the oil if you wish.

90

MEDITATE ON A MANTRA

TIME: *10–15 minutes*

INGREDIENTS: *chair or cushion*

To do meditation, it helps to have something to concentrate on in order to lead you deeper into the place of peace inside yourself. A word or mantra is a means to this end. It is a focus point. It is not possible to sit and make yourself stop thinking or go blank. The mind is only still when it has a point of focus.

Meditation means concentration. What is important for relaxation is what you concentrate on. Chances are if you concentrate on a traffic jam with fumes and angry drivers all trying to get home, your experience will be a tense one. In the same way, if you concentrate on a sunset by the sea, the nature of the tranquil scene will communicate itself to you and you will feel calm. However, we can't always be in tranquil surroundings, which is where meditation or concentration within comes into its own. Within all of us is a place of silence and of peace and using a mantra is simply one method to reach this place.

Our consciousness can be compared to an ocean. Depending on weather conditions, the visible part of the sea can be choppy, turbulent or serene without a ripple. However, no matter what is happening on the surface, if you go deep, deep, fathom-deep, there is not a wave. The bottom of the ocean is completely still and regardless of what's going on up at the top, it is unaffected.

In the same way, our mind can be compared to this ocean. Most days, we live on the surface, focused on thoughts and emotions that come and go as we are tossed about by everyday survival. Our state of mind can be determined by all sorts of changing conditions, relationships, success or failure at work, finances and so on.

The aim of inner reflection is to go deeper than these surface levels and connect up with the part of our consciousness that is untouched by all the temporary factors that come and go. To connect to the part of us, deep inside, that is constant, still and serene. It already lies within, we don't have to manufacture it. It is already there.

Through this simple meditation, spend some time with the silence within and the effects will permeate your everyday life.

METHOD

1   Sit comfortably with your back straight, in a quiet room.

2   Close your eyes and become aware of your breathing.

3   Let yourself inhale deeply and slowly without forcing the breath. As you exhale, quietly and slowly say the word 'Om', letting the saying of the word resonate until you have completely finished exhaling. You will find that as you say the end of the word, it becomes a humming sound as you exhale.

Om is commonly used for meditation for two reasons: it is a universal symbol for the life force, and it brings no specific image to mind as you say it.

4   After several minutes saying the word 'Om' as you exhale, start to internalize the word. Hear it being said in your head. It may lose its distinction as one word and become like a long hum as you mentally hear it. Allow yourself to go with this, bringing back your attention if it starts to wander away to thoughts and feelings.

5   Try to stay focused on your mantra for 15 to 20 minutes daily for maximum benefit.

91

A YOGA BREATHING TECHNIQUE

TIME: *10–15 minutes*

INGREDIENTS: *chair or cushion*

METHOD

1 Sit comfortably with the spine straight, in a quiet room where you won't be disturbed.

2 For this technique, you are going to inhale and exhale from alternate nostrils. First put your right hand up to your face. Lightly rest your right thumb on the right side of your nose.

3 Rest your index finger on your forehead and have your ring (third) or middle finger ready by the left nostril for when you need it. The hand fits quite comfortably into this position.

4 When you are ready, apply a slight pressure with the thumb, closing the right nasal passage.

Now, slowly, inhale through the left nostril, hold for two counts then apply gentle pressure on the left nostril with your middle or ring finger (releasing your thumb from the right nostril as you do so) and exhale slowly through the right nostril.

So it's breathe in through the left nostril, breathe out through the right, closing off whichever nostril is not being used with your finger or thumb.

5 Then, with the ring finger still resting on the left nostril, inhale through the right nostril, slowly, hold for two counts, then lift the ring finger from the left nostril and exhale through the left, closing the right nostril with your thumb again. In other words, breathe in through the right nostril and out through the left.

6   Try it a few times to get the movements right, then do it slowly for up to ten times. You will find that it brings about a sensation of calm and focus.

As with previous meditation techniques, the mind needs something to concentrate on. While the mind is thus distracted with alternating the breathing, it cannot be busy with thoughts or anxieties.

7   Once you have mastered the technique, you can sit and practise this breathing for 10 minutes or longer.

92

PRANAYANA BREATHING MEDITATION

TIME: *5–10 minutes*

INGREDIENTS: *chair or cushion*

This simple yogic breathing technique can be practised just about anywhere and the benefits of relaxation are immediate.

METHOD

1   Read through the technique and practise it once or twice so that you are clear what you are going to do.

2   Sit comfortably with your spine straight, either on a chair with your feet on the floor or in a cross-legged position. Rest your hands on your knees with your palms upturned and lightly join the tip of the index finger and the thumb.

3   Keep your chin level and gently stretch your neck up and forwards as though you're going to look straight ahead. Now close your eyes.

4   Breathe out through both nostrils and as you reach the end of the exhalation, pull your stomach muscles in. Hold like this for a second.

5   Now inhale as deeply as possible, feeling the air enter your abdomen, then the bottom of your lungs, then feel the air filling the tops of your lungs beneath your collar bones.

As you do this inhalation, imagine that a wave of energy is travelling up from your abdomen through the lungs up to your forehead. Hold this inhalation for two seconds. Then breathe out slowly as before, pulling the stomach muscles in again and holding for a second at the end of the exhalation. Pause for a second and start to inhale as before all the way up from the abdomen as you take the image of energy up to the forehead.

6   Continue this process for five to ten minutes. You will find that you feel relaxed and calm after doing so.

NB: It may take a few repetitions of the process before you get the hang of it but don't worry, as you practise it will become easier.

93

MEDITATE ON A CANDLE FLAME

TIME: *10–15 minutes*

INGREDIENTS: *chair or cushion, candle, matches*

METHOD

1 Sit comfortably with your spine straight either in a cross-legged position or on a chair. Rest your hands on your knees with your palms upturned and just the tip of your index finger and thumb touching.

   Have the lighting dimmed or use candles to create a soft atmosphere.

2 Position a candle a few yards from where you're sitting and focus your attention on the flame. Rest your attention there and at the same time, be aware of your breathing. Don't force your breathing, just be aware of its gentle rising and falling without controlling it.

3 Keep focusing on the flame. If you find your thoughts are coming in to distract you, don't fight them, let them come and go and keep re-focusing your attention on the flame. (As with all the other meditation techniques in the book, you need something to fix your attention on. In this case it is the candle flame.)

4 When you feel ready and your attention has been holding steadily on the flame for a short while, close your eyes and you will see the image of the flame internally. Keep focusing on it until its image fades. If you need to, reopen your eyes and repeat the process.

An image that sometimes helps people when meditating is to imagine, when you have closed your eyes, that you are in a spacious valley surrounded by mountains. You are at the centre concentrating on the image of light left from the candle flame. If thoughts come in, imagine they are like birds flying overhead. They come and they go. You don't go with them. You are focused in the centre, deeper than any temporary distractions. You are still and concentrated.

94

MEDITATE ON A MANDALA

TIME: *10–15 minutes*

INGREDIENTS: *paper, compass, pencil, paint or crayons to colour, cushion or chair*

In the East there are plenty of beautiful paintings specially created for meditation and they are called mandalas. What all these paintings have in common is that at their centre is a focal point from which the rest of the painting emerges. As with all the other techniques, the use of a mandala painting or drawing is purely to give the meditator a point to focus on so that they can become still and calm within themselves.

It is easy to create a simple mandala yourself by drawing or painting concentric circles or the centre of a flower onto a large piece of paper. You can easily draw one up with the use of a compass. The focal point is the centre of the circles or the centre of the flower.

Alternatively, if you are creative, you can do an elaborate painted or coloured drawing with shapes and patterns spiralling away from a centre point in the middle. As long as it has a clear central point, it can be used for meditation. Soft pinks or blues are a popular choice for mandala paintings.

METHOD

1   Position your mandala a comfortable distance from you so that your eyes can rest easily on the image. Some people like to do this meditation in a softly lit room so that their attention isn't too distracted by other objects or furniture in the room.

2   Sit in a comfortable position with your spine upright. Relax by breathing deeply for a few moments.

3 Focus your attention on the centre of the drawing and try to keep it there. If your attention wanders, keep bringing it back to the centre point on the drawing. If thoughts come in, let them come and go but don't pay them any attention.

4 Sit and focus for 10 to 15 minutes. Some people note that the room seems to 'shimmer', blur or grow lighter as their concentration deepens. Don't let this distract you into looking around, simply keep focused on your centre point and be aware of your breathing. You will find that the longer you concentrate on the centre point, the more tranquil you start to feel. It is a time to experience being a human being as opposed to a human doing (see Introduction). Most of the time we charge around being humans eating, humans driving, humans working, cooking, ironing and so on. This simple meditation, which allows you to experience *being* a human for as little as 10 minutes, can recharge the batteries, lower blood pressure and significantly reduce stress levels.

1. Mandala diagram drawn with a compass.

2. Make up your own mandala on a large sheet of drawing paper. Colour with paints or pastel.

95

A MEDITATION ON BREATHING AND COLOUR VISUALIZATION

TIME: *10 minutes*

INGREDIENTS: *chair or cushion, paper, crayons or paint to make colour chart*

METHOD

First read through the process so that you know what you are going to be doing.

1 Lie or sit in a comfortable position. Don't rush through the process and don't worry if you find some colours harder to envision than others.

2 Turn your focus to your breathing. Breathe deeply into your abdomen and be aware of the gentle rising and falling of the breath as you inhale and exhale. Don't force your breathing or try to control it. As you relax, it will automatically start to slow down.

3 Whilst staying aware of the rhythm of your breathing, close your eyes and start to imagine a stream of red light flowing upwards into your solar plexus. Keep visualizing this for a minute, then see the light changing to orange.

4 Keep breathing slowly and rhythmically as you do this and keep imagining the orange for at least one minute. Now see the orange light become lighter and change to yellow, flooding up and into the solar plexus at a gentle unhurried pace. Spend about one minute on the yellow light.

5 Now the colour changes again. Imagine green light flowing into the same area but this time it is coming from directly in front of you.

Spend a minute breathing steadily as the image of green light flows gently into the solar plexus. Spend a minute on this.

After the green, the colours are going to come from the air above you starting with blue. Spend a minute imagining that a stream of blue light is flowing steadily into you as you breathe deeply.

6 After a minute see the blue colour change into indigo.

7 After another minute, visualize the stream of light becoming violet. Spend at least one minute on this.

By now you should have been visualizing for eight or nine minutes.

8 When you have been through all the colours, see yourself as being bathed in blue light. When you are ready, open your eyes.

If it helps you to remember the order of colours, you could draw sections on a piece of paper and colour in each section according to the sequence. Keep the paper handy so that if you need to, you can open your eyes and remind yourself which colour is next.

THE SEQUENCE (TO BE DONE AS YOU BREATHE SLOWLY AND STEADILY)

1 Red
Orange   flowing upwards into the solar plexus
Yellow

2 Green   flowing into the solar plexus from directly in front of you

3 Blue
Indigo   flowing into the solar plexus from the air above you
Violet

4 Finally, imagine you are being bathed in blue light.

96

A BUDDHIST MEDITATION

'Mindfully he breathes in, mindfully he breathes out.'

The Buddha

TIME: *15–30 minutes*

INGREDIENTS: *none necessary*

The following Vipassana meditation is derived from the school of Theravadin Buddhism and is believed by many people to be the original method that the Buddha himself taught.

The aim of the meditation is to achieve stillness through concentration on the ingoing and outgoing of the breath. It will strengthen the power of concentration and bring whoever practises it completely into the present moment. The breath is like an anchor for the here and now; although our consciousness may be preoccupied with the past or the future, the breath is always present. If it wasn't, we wouldn't be alive.

Few people live in the here and now because thoughts, goals, dreams or memories occupy so much of our attention, making us think about past occurrences, future deadlines, appointments and plans. How often do we wish away the week at work looking forward to the weekend? Or spend a day at work wishing it were home time? So often happiness lies at any time but the present moment. For example, I will be happy when . . . I go on holiday, get a new car, fall in love, have a child, get a job I like, move house, get this situation over with; or alternatively, I was happy when . . . I was young, I was with so and so, I was in the Caribbean last year. And so the days roll by and we miss and wish away the only time that is real – the present.

It is only in the present that true happiness lies and this meditation is a technique to bring your awareness to a point of stillness where you can appreciate the perfection in the moment.

METHOD

1   Sit in a quiet room in a comfortable and relaxed position and close your eyes.

2   Become aware of your breathing by either of two methods. Both of the following are equally effective for this meditation, but choose only one of them.

Either:

a) Focus your attention on the breath as it enters the tip of your nostrils, the cold air being breathed in, the warm air being breathed out. Don't attempt to follow the breath down to the lungs but stay with your attention fixed on the nostrils like a sentry at a gate watching and noting who is entering and who is leaving.

or

b) Focus your attention on the rise and fall of the abdomen as you inhale and exhale. Don't attempt to follow the breath up or down, simply stay with your awareness fixed on the motion of the abdomen as the breathing happens.

Whichever method you choose, watch your breath with total awareness. As you concentrate on either of these methods, after a time, you will start to feel yourself becoming still.

3   As the sensation of stillness grows, while being aware of your focal point (i.e. either the tip of the nostrils or the abdomen), also let yourself be aware of your body and how it feels. Starting with the face, then the head, the arms, the body, the legs, the feet then returning to your point of focus at either the nostrils or the abdomen. As the sensation of being still within yourself grows you will find that you can experience a sense of profound peace and acute awareness of being completely present in the moment.

97
PRAY

TIME: *as long as you like*

Prayer can bring about a feeling of great serenity and emotional release for believers and non-believers alike. Don't miss out, because of cynicism or doubt, on the peace of mind that can come over you after a moment's prayer. Put it on hold for a few minutes and if you can't come to terms with praying to a God of your understanding, see it as time to talk to your higher self or the life force or energy behind everything.

Prayer is talking to God, meditation is listening. When you pray, you let your heart or the deeper part of yourself speak through and be heard.

So much of our time is spent in our heads. Planning how to live to work and work to live, carrying responsibility and anxiety about plain survival – mortgages, children, careers, threat of redundancies, illness, pensions. To take time out to talk as though there is a power listening can be very therapeutic. Whatever comes up, say it, because to let go of our egos and for a short time to assume a smaller position in relation to the Universe can bring a wonderful sense of calm. Take time to acknowledge that we are but a small speck in a house, in a job, in a city, in a country, in a continent, in a world in time and space that for all our sophistication and technological advancement, we still know so little about. Pause for a moment from the rush of our hurried existence and just be, a soul in an enormous universe where, although there is much to appreciate and be glad about, there is also so much bad news, catastrophes, heartache and so many things out of control that we don't understand.

Much of the time in life, logic and reason rule. To admit ignorance, that you don't know, can be seen as a sign of failure. This is one time that you can let it all out. Put your reason on hold and let the deeper part through. Some people are surprised by the intensity of feeling that emerges, emotions, anger, sadness which perhaps have been pushed down as we battle on.

Although theoretically you can pray anywhere, churches, temples and prayer halls do have an atmosphere of calm about them which can be absorbed by a short visit. Places of worship are tranquil. So much of the time we live in a world of noise, traffic, chatter, radios, phones, television. In fact, people avoid silence, filling it with sound. Churches and temples are silent and that constitutes a large part of their calming influence. In the quiet atmosphere, you can be alone with your thoughts, close down from the world and simply pour out whatever you need or want to say.

Let whatever words that come to mind form your prayer, whether it be of thanks, or of your need for help or guidance, or for a recognition that there is some good out there amidst the ever-growing madness. Don't worry about the right words.

Prayers can be short or long, be from books or of your own making, whatever feels most natural to you. If you find it hard to find the words yourself, read through inspirational books until you find a prayer that expresses how you feel. When you pray, as Kahlil Gibran said, 'you rise to meet in the air those who are praying at that very hour, and whom save in prayer you may not meet.'

PRAYER EXAMPLES

1   Grant me the serenity to accept the things I cannot change,
The courage to change the things I can,
And the wisdom to know the difference.

2   An Indian prayer
O great Spirit, whose voice I hear in the winds
and whose breath gives life to the world.
Hear me. I am small and weak
I need your strength and wisdom
Let me walk in beauty,
And make my eyes ever behold the red and purple sunset,
Make my hands respect the things you have made and my ears sharp to hear your voice.
Make me wise so that I may understand the things you have taught my people

Let me learn the lessons you have hidden in every leaf and rock
I seek strength, not to be greater than my brother, but to fight my
greatest enemy – myself.
Make me ready to come to you with clean hands and straight eyes
And when life fades, as the fading sunset
May my spirit come to you without shame.

(Written by Kateri Tekakuitha (1656–1680), a North American
Indian, also known as Lily of the Mohawks.)

98

FOLLOW YOUR HEART

TIME: *unlimited*

In this day and age, a statement like follow your heart may seem impossible or even irresponsible. However, I felt it was important to put it in this section of the book as to go against or ignore your heart's desires can be a major cause of much of life's stress.

Often we choose the familiar or comfortable because we know the territory, want as little confrontation as possible and want to live life quietly and peacefully, whereas following your heart can involve risks, challenges and the unfamiliar. If you're truly happy and relaxed in your life then fine, disregard this, but for those who know that there is something that you want to do, but that takes perhaps a leap of faith, confrontation and uncertainty, then I say do it.

Paulo Coelho in his book *The Alchemist* (1988) writes that if you follow your heart the whole universe conspires to make your wish possible. (Note he doesn't write easy, but possible.) It is often through taking risks that we are stretched, that we grow and evolve as beings and surely that's part of our reason to be here – to keep learning.

To stay still is to stagnate and there's nothing more stressful or debilitating than that.

Kahlil Gibran in *The Prophet* (1923) writes:

> When love beckons to you, follow him
> Though his ways are hard and steep.
> And when his wings enfold you, yield to him,
> though the sword hidden amongst his pinions may wound you.
> And when he speaks to you believe in him,
> though his voice may shatter your dreams as the north wind lays waste the
> garden.

For even as love crowns you so he shall crucify you.

Even as he is for your growth so is he for your pruning.

Even as he ascends to your height and caresses your tenderest branches
that quiver in the sun,

So shall he descend to your roots and shake them in their clinging to the
earth.

Like sheaves of corn he gathers you unto himself.

He threshes you to make you naked.

He sifts you to free you from your husks.

He grinds you to whiteness.

He kneads you until you are pliant,

And then he assigns you to his sacred fire, that you may

become sacred bread for God's sacred fire.

And all these things shall love do unto you that you may know the secrets
of your heart, and in that knowledge become a fragment of life's heart.

But if in your fear you would seek only love's pleasure,

Then it is better for you that you cover your nakedness and pass out of
love's threshing floor,

Into the seasonless world where you shall laugh, but not all of your
laughter and weep but not all of your tears.

To follow your heart doesn't necessarily mean throw in your job or abandon your responsibilities. It means make time for growth, take time to learn new skills. More than anything, strive to keep learning about this mysterious life and universe that we live in. Follow your dreams. Don't become bitter, closed or cynical, don't stifle your soul. Make manifest your dreams. Don't ever give up. Stay open with both mind and heart to all sorts of possibilities.

99

MAKE TIME FOR WHAT INSPIRES YOU TO BELIEVE IN THE POSSIBILITY OF A HIGHER POWER

TIME: *as per individual*

INGREDIENTS: *variable on personal preferences*

Recognize what inspires you and find time for this in your life. This is the only method that is variable because it is down to personal preference. I include it here because it is an important part of the relaxation package.

When the soul is empty, nothing is right. Inspiration is food for the soul. We all need it, yet so often it is easy to go about our existence, working to live and living to work, caught up in the humdrum of survival with no time to stand back and enjoy the simple pleasures of life or stand in awe at the mystery of it all.

So often happiness lies in the future: I will be happy when I go on holiday, get a pay rise, find the love of my life, have a baby etc. In the meantime, we miss the here and now, the present, the only time that is real and it is only in this moment that we can ever experience a sense of true happiness or joy.

A German philosopher called Rudolf Otto wrote a book called *The Idea of the Holy* (1923). He wrote about moments that are sacred, rare times of quiet joy, when you can see that all is right with the world, get a glimpse of the perfection amidst the chaos, the magic amidst the madness. He called these experiences that draw us right into the present moment the numinous. He said different catalysts trigger off this wonderful feeling in different people. For some it is a piece of music or art, for others a pastoral scene – a sunrise or sunset. Some perhaps find it in meditation or in being in a holy place, for others it comes about from being creative or dancing.

These moments of simple yet profound appreciation can do wonders for anyone who is so caught up in the stresses of survival that they are missing the magic all around.

Make time to do whatever it takes to let your soul soar and feel glad to simply be alive by being in the moment. Find out what is the 'numinous' for you, what brings you into the moment, what works for you, inspires you as an individual, whether it be meditation, prayer, a piece of music, dance, a sacred place, a walk in a forest or simply gardening.

100

TAKE COMFORT IN A PIECE OF INSPIRATIONAL WRITING

TIME: *3 minutes*

Sometimes just reading an inspired piece of writing can put things back in perspective. If you haven't your own favourite already tucked away somewhere, try one of the pieces below.

DESIDERATA

Go placidly in the noise and haste and remember what peace there may be in silence. As far as possible without surrender be on good terms with all persons. Speak your truth quietly and clearly, and listen to the others, even the dull and ignorant, they too have their story. Avoid loud and aggressive persons, they are vexations to the spirit. If you compare yourself with others, you may become vain and bitter, for always there will be greater and lesser persons than yourself. Enjoy your achievements as well as your plans. Keep interested in your own career, however humble, it is a real possession in the changing fortunes of time. Exercise caution in your business affairs, for the world is full of trickery. But let this not blind you to what virtue there is, many persons strive for high ideals, and everywhere life is full of heroism.

Be yourself, especially do not feign affection. Neither be cynical about love, for in the face of all aridity and disenchantment, it is as perennial as the grass. Take kindly the council of years, gracefully surrendering the things of youth. Nurture strength of spirit to shield you in sudden misfortune. But do not distress yourself with imaginings. Many fears are born of fatigue and loneliness. Beyond a wholesome discipline, be gentle with yourself. You are a child of the universe, no less than the trees and the stars, you have a right to be here. And whether or not it is clear to you, no doubt the universe is unfolding as it should. Therefore be at peace with God, whatever you perceive him to be, and whatever your labors and aspirations, in the noisy confusion of life keep peace with your soul. With all its sham, drudgery and broken dreams, it is still a beautiful world. Be careful. Strive to be happy.

(*Found in Old Saint Paul's Church, Baltimore dated 1692*)

Two other alternatives are a piece taken from *The Prophet* by Kahlil Gibran (1923) and verses 25–34 of Mathew Chapter 6 in the New Testament.

Your pain is the breaking of the shell that encloses your understanding. Even as the stone of the fruit must break, that its heart may stand in the sun, so must you know pain.
And could you keep your heart in wonder at the daily miracles of your life, your pain would not seem less wondrous than your joy,
And you would accept the seasons of your heart, even as you have always accepted the seasons that pass over your fields.
And you would watch with serenity through the winters of your grief.
Much of your pain is self chosen.
It is the bitter potion by which the physician within you heals your sick self.
Therefore trust the physician, and drink his remedy in silence and tranquillity:
For his hand, though heavy and hard, is guided by the tender hand of the Unseen.
And the cup he brings, though it may burn your lips, has been fashioned of the clay which the Potter has moistened with his own sacred tears.

Kahlil Gibran

FROM THE BIBLE, MATTHEW CHAPTER 6, VERSES 25–34 IN THE NEW TESTAMENT

Therefore I say unto you, Take no thought for your life, what ye shall eat, or what ye shall drink, nor yet for your body, what ye shall put on. Is not the life more than meat, and the body more than raiment?

Behold the birds of the air, for they sow not, neither do they reap, nor gather into barns, yet your heavenly father feedeth them. Are ye not much better than they? And why take ye thought for raiment? Consider the lilies of the field, how they grow, they toil not, neither do they spin.

And yet I say to you, that even Solomon in all his glory was not arrayed like one of these.

Wherefore if God so clothe the grass of the field, which today is, and tomorrow is cast into the oven, shall he not much more clothe you, O ye of little faith?

Therefore take no thought, saying What shall we eat? or What shall we drink? or wherewithal shall we be clothed? for your heavenly Father knoweth that you have need of all these things. But seek ye first the kingdom of God, and his righteousness, and all these things shall be added unto you.

Take therefore no thought for the morrow, for the morrow shall take thought for the things itself.

101

BE YOURSELF

Finally, I'm going to end on some of the best advice anyone ever gave me.

Be yourself.
The best become the best by being themselves.
Don't ever try and copy anyone
or walk in anybody else's footsteps.
The best become the best by being themselves.
So relax.
And be yourself.
Guru Maharaji

USEFUL ADDRESSES

From shortcut 4
For more information try:
British Association for Autogenic
Training and Therapy
18, Holtsmere Close
Garston
Watford
WD2 6NE
Tel: 01923 675501

From shortcut 16
For further information about the
Alexander technique:
Society of Teachers of Alexander
Technique
20, London House
266 Fulham Road
London
SW10 9EL
Tel: 0171 352 0828

From shortcut 18
The Sitting Partner is available
from:
Back in Action
PO Box 559
Bourne End
Bucks
SL8 5RL

From shortcuts 26, 85
Relaxation tapes: mail order
Tel: 0198 678 1682

New World
Paradise Farm
Westhall
Halesworth
Suffolk
IP19 8RH

From shortcut 28
The Backstretcher is available
from:
ENANEF Ltd
63, New Inn Lane
Guildford
GU4 7HT
Tel: 01483 33276

or from:
Back in Action
PO Box 559
Bourne End
Bucks
SL8 5RL

From shortcut 29
For details of the hydrotherapy bath:
Ben Bates Hydro-Bath
Sandy Farm
Sands Road
The Sands
Farnham
Surrey
GU10 1PX
Tel: 01252 781231

or from:
Balsan Hydrotherapy
Crowden-Naylor Associates Ltd
112, St Mary's Road
Market Harborough
Leicestershire
LE16 7DX
Tel: 01858 468469

From shortcuts 32, 33, 34, 35, 36, 37, 38

For vitamin and minerals:
Nature's Best
1, Lamberts Road
Tunbridge Wells
TN2 3EQ
Tel: 01892 513116

From shortcut 42

Suppliers of herbs:
East West Herb Shop
3 Neal's Yard
Covent Garden
London
WC2H 9DP

To find a qualified herbalist in
your area, send SAE to:
Secretary
National Institute of Herbalists
9 Palace Gate
Exeter
Devon
EX1 1JA

From shortcuts 45, 69

For details of kinesiology and a
list of practitioners send large
SAE to:
Secretary
ASK
39, Brown's Rd
Surbiton
Surrey
KT5 8ST

From shortcut 49

You can obtain a wheat bag from:
The Original Wheat Bag Company Ltd
PO Box 437
Woking
Surrey
GU21 4FU
Tel/Fax: 01276 857556

From shortcut 50

Essential Balm can be obtained
from:
Man Shuen Hong (London)
4, Tring Close
Barkingside
Ilford
Essex
IG2 7LQ
Tel: 0181 554 3838

For shortcuts 51, 52, 54, 55, 58, 59, 60, 63, 89
Aromatherapy oils by mail order:
Fleur Aromatherapy
Pembroke Studios
Pembroke Road
London
N10 2JE
Tel: 0181 444 7424
Fax: 0181 444 0704

From shortcut 53
For more information about homoeopathy:
The British Homoeopathic Association
27A Devonshire Street
London
WC1N 1RJ
Tel: 0171 935 2163

or from:
The Hahnemann Society
Humane Education Centre
Bounds Green Road
London
N22 4EV
Tel: 0181 889 1595

From shortcuts 57, 62
For more information about shiatsu or practitioners:
The Shiatsu Society
14, Oakdene Road
Redhill
Surrey
RH1 6BT
Tel: 01737 767896

From shortcut 64
For more information on reflexology:
International Institute of Reflexology
Francis Wagg, UK Director
15 Hatfield Close
Tonbridge
Kent
TN10 4JP
Tel: 01732 350629

From shortcut 65
You can get a foot roller from:
Shakti Chakra
PO Box 3984
London
SE12 0EJ
Tel: 0956 233694

From shortcut 66
For a list of local aromatherapists:
International Federation of Aromatherapists (IFA)
Stamford House
2/4 Chiswick High Road
London
W4 1TH
Tel: 0181 742 2605

or from:
Aromatherapy Organisations Council (AOC)
3 Latymer Close
Braybrooke
Market Harborough
Leicester
LE16 8LN
Tel: 01858 434242

From shortcut 67

For information about the
Aromatherapy Steam Tube:
Consumer Technology Services Ltd
Providence Place
Wyke
Bradford
BD12 8BJ
Tel: 01274 676567
Fax: 01274 693987

From shortcut 68

For information on flotation tanks
and centres:
The International Flotation and
Stress Research Association
21, Bond Street
Brighton
BN1 1RD

or from:
The Flotation Tank Association
3A Elms Crescent
London
SW4 8QE

From shortcut number 70

For information about where to
find a local counsellor:
The Westminster Pastoral
Foundation
23, Kensington Square
London
W8 5HN

or from:
The British Association of
Counselling
37a Sheep Street
Rugby
Warwickshire
CV21 3BX

From shortcut 73

For more information about art
therapy:
British Association of Art
Therapies
11A, Richmond Road
Brighton
BN2 3RL

Dance therapy:
The Arts Therapies Dept
Springfield Hospital
Glenburnie Road
London
SW17 7DJ

Music therapy:
The Association of Professional
Music Therapists
The Meadow
68, Pierce Lane
Fulbourn
Cambs
CB1 5DL

or from:
The British Society for Music
Therapists
69, Avondale Ave
East Barnet
Herts
EN4 8NB

Drama therapy:
The British Association for Drama
Therapists
The Old Mill
Tolpuddle
Dorchester
Dorset
DT2 7EX

From shortcut 78

For details of light boxes and
natural alarm clocks:
Outside In (Cambridge) Ltd
Unit 21
Scotland Road Estate
Dry Drayton
Cambridge
CB3 8AT
Tel: 0954 211955

From shortcut 80

For information about beds:
Concern for Comfort
Abacus House
Manor Road
London
W13 0AS
Tel: 0181 810 9508

From shortcut 81

Orthopaedic pillows are available
from:
Back in Action
PO Box 559
Bourne End
Bucks
SL8 5RL

or from:
John Mills Ltd
72, Albert Street
London
NW1 7NR
Tel: 0171 388 7212

From shortcut 83

For details about chairs:
Back in Action
PO Box 559
Bourne End
Bucks
SL8 5RL

Wave Seats are obtainable from:
The Wave Seat Company
Riverside Workshop
Forge Lane
Keswick
Cumbria
CA12 4NX
Tel: 017687 73612

From shortcut number 86

For more information about Feng
Shui:
Graham Gunn
FSS
18, Alacross Rd
London
W5 4HT
0181 567 2043

From shortcut 88

Pets As Therapy (PAT)
4–6 New Road
Ditton
Kent
ME20 6AD

INDEX